KU-024-330

Acknowledgements

Whilst two of us are credited as the authors of this book, its creation has been a team effort. In particular we would like to thank Manda Freeman for so diligently proof reading the early manuscripts, Jacqueline Cole for researching the first tranche of facts that make up the left hand pages and Jason Hopper for designing the page layouts and cover to a standard rarely seen in book publishing.

A wider team were kind enough to read the finished book and encouraged us to print the first edition, thanks goes to Elizabeth Vaughton, Dave Gooderidge, Karen West, Rebecca Megaw, Nick Webb, Laura Wells, Michelle Guy, Jane Mole, the incredibly thorough Tracey Thake along with Bex Keer, Antonie Fountain and Bram Dekker at Stop the Traffik.

We are also very grateful to those people in our lives who have shown us the value of trust, either by placing their trust in us or by honouring the trust we've placed in them.

"When I trust someone I confer value on them"

Dave Gooderidge

TRUST
UNWRAPPED

A STORY OF ETHICS, INTEGRITY AND CHOCOLATE

First Published in 2008 by Fresh Publishing

A CIP catalogue record for this book is available from the British Library

ISBN 978-0-955802-40-9

Typset and design by District-6   www.district-6.com
Printed and bound in Great Britain by Biddles Ltd, King's Lynn, Norfolk

Fresh Publishing
PO Box 101
WARE
SG11 1WA
England

www.freshgroup.co.uk

For my father Nigel, dependable,
faithful and trustworthy

Dan Collins

For mum Jeanette,
who taught me to trust

David Thompson

Introduction

This book is different from most business manuals, hopefully as it's more fun to read, more concise, not stuffy and full of truth.

Sometimes the thought of wading through an academic tome is too much and we are tempted to relax with a novel instead, feeling slightly guilty that we aren't keeping up with the latest management thinking. In *Trust Unwrapped* we use the time-honoured medium of story to put across our message, supported by easy to reference facts, quotes and news items on the left-hand pages.

So if you have a couple of hours spare while you wait for a flight or sit on a train, enjoy the story. If on the other hand you are rushing to find some data to back up a presentation or training session then spend ten minutes scanning these pages and see if the book can outperform Google!

Trust n.&v.

1. (a) a firm belief in the reliability of truth
   or strength etc. of a person or thing
   (b) the state of being relied on

2. (a) a confident expectation

3. (a) a thing or person committed
   to one's care
   (b) the resulting obligation or
   responsibility (OED)

Prologue

Eight year old Laura skipped through the grounds of her parents garden, the layers of her taffeta dress rustling as she moved.

She started to make her way up the tree that would lead her to her favourite place and from where she could survey the entire garden. Taking care to place her hands and feet carefully to make sure that she didn't fall, before long she reached her destination. She stopped for a moment to catch her breath, and looked out at the landscape below her.

Confidently, Laura looked above her and saw that there was still further to climb. Without so much as a second thought, she hitched up her layered dress and started to clamber up. In fact, she climbed higher and higher. When she finally stopped, Laura steadied herself to see how far she had come. She panicked. She felt butterflies in her tummy. It was a long way down. She could see safe ground way below her, and wished with all her might that she was still there. Overcome with emotion, her bottom lip started to quiver. Before long, she was in floods of tears.

Her sobs were soon punctuated with screams of "Daddy, Daddy, Daddy!"

Sure enough, her father John came to rescue her. He stood at the bottom of the tree and shouted his daughter's name. He could hear her but he couldn't see her.

"Daddy, I'm up here!"

Laura rustled the branches to draw attention to herself. Her father took a step back in order to see his little princess. He tutted to himself, as if to say 'I told her not to climb that far', but he knew this was not the time for reprimand. Despite the bravery that it would have taken for her to be so adventurous, Laura was now clearly very scared.

The oak tree had stood in the centre of the garden since the Andersons' house was built in 1800. It was, without doubt, the focal point of the garden. Laura's father stood underneath the part of the tree where his daughter was stuck. Her sobs were tempered by the reassuring sight of her father. He smiled up at her, and she smiled back, wiping the tears from her face with the sleeve of her top.

Laura was a typical girl of her age except that, growing up with three brothers, she had developed strong determination and a competitive streak. She was always pushing herself to be better, faster, in an effort to catch up with her brothers. She was determined not to be left behind when they went out to play. Occasionally, that determination would get her into sticky situations. This was one such occasion.

"Look at you!" said John, encouragingly. "You've climbed such a long way!

Laura smiled nervously, her confidence returning.

"Ok, Laura, now I can't come up there and get you because I'm too big, so I need you to shuffle out onto that big branch. Can you do that for me, darling?"

Laura nodded and, very slowly but surely, with words of encouragement from her father on the ground beneath her, did just that. Before long she was sitting on a large branch that was directly above the grass. She hung on tight. Her father stood directly beneath the branch and reached his arms up towards his daughter.

"That's it, good girl, Laura. Now I'm right here, all you have to do is jump, and I'll catch you."

"Daddy, I don't want to, I'm scared."

"I know you are, sweetheart, but I'll catch you, I promise. You've got nothing to worry about."

Laura clutched the branch. It looked such a long way down. She sat, scared and shaking, on the branch.

"Just take a deep breath, close your eyes, and I'll catch you" repeated her father.

"What if you drop me? Don't drop me!" said Laura, nervously.

"I won't drop you, I promise. Trust me, Laura. I won't drop you. I'll catch you nice and tight. Trust me."

That was all the reassurance that she needed. Of course she trusted her father, and her mother, more than anyone in the world. She knew that they would never let her down. That was it, her mind was made up. She prepared herself for a moment and then closed her eyes. Her father, standing below her, knew what was coming.

Laura jumped, with nothing but trust to break her fall.

"Miss Anderson? Yes, we've been expecting you. Please come this way." The Maître D' nodded regally at Laura and Tom and led them into the main restaurant. Walking behind the immaculately dressed Maître D', Laura held Tom's hand and smiled in response to the other diners who looked up from their conversations as the young couple were led to their table. Tom looked nervous. The restaurant was magnificent. It was a large room with high ceilings which gave it a deserving dramatic feel. The intricate baroque murals on the walls and ceiling were edged in gilt, which glistened in the light cast by the grandiose crystal chandeliers. The copious number of French waiters all dressed in starched white jackets completed the scene. This was clearly a 'you've arrived' restaurant. Laura and Tom had never been anywhere like this before. Being used to the student cafeteria at university, and Pizza Express 'for special occasions', this was something else. As they reached their table, waiting staff seemed to spring from nowhere to pull out Laura and Tom's chairs, arrange their crisp linen napkins on their laps, pour water and proffer opened menus. Laura and Tom looked at each other while the staff bustled around them, and waited for the staff to move out of earshot before they dared speak.

Laura leaned forward. "You look very handsome" she whispered to her boyfriend, in a thinly veiled attempt to help him feel comfortable in the intimidating surroundings. Tom spent so much time in uniform, Laura had almost forgotten how smart he could look when he made the effort. And he had clearly made a considerable effort for their special occasion; he wanted to make sure that they had an evening to remember.

Tom smiled. "This is the poshest place I've ever been to!" he said quietly, leaning forward to make sure that he wasn't overheard.

Laura giggled. "I know – me too. Special though, isn't it?"

Tom nodded. "Oh yeah, very nice, very nice."

The couple reached for their menus and sat for a moment while they perused the options.

"I guess bangers and mash is out, then!" said Tom, looking up from the menu. Laura smiled.

'Yes, looks like it!"

A waiter approached with his order book in hand, and they made their decisions.

"Perhaps you would like some wine?" asked the waiter politely.

Tom and Laura looked at each other. 'I think it'll have to be Champagne as we're celebrating."

The waiter nodded. "Congratulations. Veuve Clicquot is our house Champagne, ma'am?"

"I'm sure that will be fine," replied Laura and, with a gracious nod and a step back from the table, the waiter was on his way.

Top 5 most trusted professions

Profession	% responding 'trusted a great deal/quite a lot'
1. Firefighters	95%
2. Airline Pilots	92%
3. Pharmacists	89%
4. Nurses	86%
5. Doctors	85%

Results from the 2007 Readers Digest Trusted Brands Survey of over 24,000 residents of Europe

"Champagne, eh?" said Tom cheekily. "Didn't fancy a pint of cider, then?"

The two laughed at the incredulity of ordering a pint of cider at The Ritz.

"I'm so proud of you, Laura, you've done so well."

"So have you – you'll make more difference to the world than I will" she said, taking his hand. She loved Tom dearly. They had met in Freshers' week at university and had hit it off straightaway. She admired his honesty, and he was undoubtedly the most caring and giving man that she had ever met. She was very happy with Tom, and he with her. They made a good couple. Friends would often use the 'opposites attract' maxim when they talked about Tom and Laura, and there was a great deal of truth in that observation. Whereas Tom was someone who was happy with his lot in life, Laura was indeed quite the opposite. She had been Head Girl in her last year at school, and had attended university with the intention of coming away with a First in her business administration degree. It was no surprise to anyone who knew Laura that she achieved this goal. Just like she achieved every goal that she set herself. Tom was focused, but in a different sense. His sole ambition in life was to become a firefighter and to have a family that he loved. His ambitions may have been simpler than his girlfriend's but they were no less important. Despite their different views of the world, Laura and Tom's relationship just seemed to work.

"Well, I guess so, but you'll make more money!"

"That is true" she smiled.

"A handshake is good enough for me -
anyway it's all being videoed."

"I'm different from you. I've always wanted to be a firefighter. To think that I'll be able to help people, to save people, to save lives even. It's just what I've always wanted to do – I can't explain it."

"And you've done so well to get on the fire service trainee scheme – how many people applied again?"

"I think about a thousand people applied for 30 places." Tom smiled to himself – it was beginning to dawn on him that he was very fortunate to be selected, and that this was quite an achievement – one that he had every right to be proud of.

The waiter arrived with the Champagne. After showing Laura the orange label he poured a small amount for her to try. Though she didn't know what she was tasting for, she duly did as she was asked and gave an appreciative nod. The waiter smiled approvingly and began to fill the couple's glasses. Tom and Laura sat and watched the bubbles float up the glass, waiting until the waiter had filled their glasses and left them to their conversation.

"Cheers – here's to you." Laura raised her glass and tipped it subtly in Tom's direction. He did the same and the couple clinked their glasses, being careful not to do so too loudly for fear of attracting the attention of their fellow diners.

"And to you!" said Tom, half whispering.

Laura smiled appreciatively.

"I mean, look at you – little Miss Corporate!" joked Tom.

"Oi, watch it!"

"Well, you are – how many people get a Brand Manager

Brand Trust

A brand is more than a product itself. Good brand guardians spend effort in creating and informing consumers about the correct attitudes and behaviours of their brand. The relationship between a brand and its consumers has become increasingly complex in recent years as consumers have easy access to more knowledge than they used to, and the internet allows for straightforward comparisons between products.

Brand trust is one element of brand image since trust is a vital ingredient in generating a bond between a consumer and a brand.

job straight out of university, eh? And with a starting salary that's more than I'll ever earn as a firefighter. And a brand new Ford Focus." Laura wasn't sure if she detected a hint of envy in Tom's voice.

She smiled softly at her boyfriend. "Yes, I suppose you're right. Hey – it'll mean that we can get a nicer apartment, though. And if I reach my targets and get a bonus, we can take our first proper holiday. How nice would that be?"

Tom relaxed back into his chair. "That would be really cool – somewhere warm, where the water's blue and the white sandy beaches stretch for miles" he said dreamily.

"I was thinking of somewhere more glamorous than Blackpool!" joked Laura.

They both laughed, just as the waiters arrived with their starters.

As Tom picked up his fork and gently prodded his warm chicken salad, he looked up at Laura. "Just promise me that you won't get sucked into the corporate life thing and forget about what's important. Promise me you won't change." There was an intensity in Tom's voice that Laura hadn't heard before. Laura could tell that this was clearly important to him.

She squeezed Tom's hand lovingly across the table as she looked deep into his eyes.

"Of course not, my darling," she said softly.

But deep down, with what she had in mind, Laura wasn't quite sure that was a promise she was going to be able to keep.

66 *Trust yourself. Create the kind of self that you will be happy to live with all your life. Make the most of yourself by fanning the tiny inner sparks of possibility into flames of achievement.* **99**

Golda Meir, Former Prime Minister of Israel

Laura had bought a new suit for her first day in her first proper job after leaving university. All her friends were amazed that she managed to get a Brand Manager role as her first job, when most of them were on traineeships of varying shapes and sizes – even those who were joining professional firms. Laura felt very proud as she walked into the offices of Gabriels Foods for the first time as a bona fide employee. Whilst at university, Laura had taken a temporary role there during her term breaks. She had fitted in well, enjoying her work immensely, to the extent that she was deadset on Gabriels as her employer of choice once she had graduated. Despite being here countless times before, this time she was walking in as an employee. As a Brand Manager, no less. She smiled as she approached the Reception desk.

"Hi, I'm Laura Anderson. I start this morning as a Brand Manager."

"Ah yes, good morning, Laura, JJ said that you were starting with us this morning – it's lovely to meet you!"

Laura was pleased, if a little surprised, to get such a warm welcome.

"Take a seat – he'll be down in just a second."

Laura sat in the reception area and took in her environment. There were framed posters all over the walls of a selection

The Readers Digest 2007 Trusted Brands Survey

In the UK, the following brands have proved to be consistent winners every year since the survey began in 2001.

Category	Brand
Automotive	Ford
Kitchen appliances	Hotpoint
Internet service	AOL
Mobile phone handset	Nokia
Camera	Canon
Holiday tour company	Thomson
Bank/Building Society	Lloyds TSB
Analgesic/pain relief	Nurofen
Soap powder	Persil

of Gabriel's products, both old and new, and many photographs of JJ Gabriel with various dignitaries, including The Queen who opened their new factory wing five years ago. Gabriels was a successful global company, having grown significantly under the leadership of JJ Gabriel, the vivacious, entrepreneurial son of the founder, who bequeathed the business to JJ some 20 years ago. Gabriels was a key employer locally and had an exceptionally good name, not only in the local community but also in the rest of the country. Their business was confectionery. Chocolate in all shapes and sizes, many of which were household names. JJ would travel the world searching for new exotic flavours which resulted in their continuing reputation for product innovation. However, the core of their business was their stable of familiar products that were used by everyone – they were a well-loved household name in the UK. They were particularly well-known for the catchphrase that they tagged on to all their products in the festive season: 'Christmas wouldn't be Christmas without Gabriels'. This clever piece of marketing had embedded itself in the psyche of the country to the extent that people used variations of it in conversation, in a similar way to those other classic advertising taglines such as 'it does exactly what it says on the tin' and 'a dog is for life, not just for Christmas' had done. Laura distinctly remembered her father making bread sauce (which everyone in the family hated, except him) every Christmas Day, and how he would add it to the table that was already bursting with food with a jovial 'Christmas wouldn't be Christmas without bread sauce'.

Consumer Trust

Consumers' trust in companies and organisations is incredibly complex. The National Consumer Council identifies consistent factors that contribute to the perception of trust:

- Being a large national organisation for some types of purchase and being a small or family business for other types of purchase
- Being well-established
- Being well-known

A good reputation encompasses:

- Quality, reliability, value for money and efficiency of service
- Well trained, knowledgeable and friendly staff willing to offer unbiased advice
- Good after-sales service
- Offering added value
- Being perceived not to be too successful
- Effective marketing and frequent exposure
- Use of kitemarks or Trade Association symbols

Each year he would say it, and each year Laura and her brothers would roll their eyes in loving disdain. It became as much a part of Christmas as Christmas itself. Gabriels was already a part of her life, and she was proud that she was going to be a part of the future of this company that played such an intimate part in people's lives.

"Laura!"

Laura almost jumped out of her skin. JJ had arrived.

"Oh, JJ, I was miles away – it's good to see you."

Her larger than life new boss grabbed her firmly by the arm and gave her an affectionate kiss on each cheek.

"And good to see you, my dear – I'm delighted that you've finally started – I've been so looking forward to having you join the team."

Laura was beaming with pride. As a student working through the holidays, she had come into contact with JJ just once. He, on the other hand, had kept a close eye on the young woman who had been highlighted to him as someone with 'stand out' talent, and one to watch for the future. Whilst unbeknownst to Laura, this would explain the exceptionally warm welcome she received from her new Boss.

"Well, thank you, that's very kind, I can't wait to get started!" JJ's enthusiasm was infectious.

JJ led Laura into the offices and spent the next couple of hours personally showing her around the production factory, the offices, the packaging plant, and the staff recreation areas that he had added just a couple of years ago. Laura was particularly impressed with the state-

"OKAY, SIMMS, WE HAVE A VERBAL AGREEMENT, BUT I'D LIKE MY LAWYER TO CHECK IT OUT."

of-the-art gym and swimming pool. She spared a brief thought for Tom, whose 'recreation' area at the fire station consisted of a small nicotine stained room that hadn't been decorated since the 1970s, with nothing but a small portable television and melamine furniture as home comforts. She couldn't believe her luck – she had certainly fallen on her feet with this job.

"I believe it's important that we treat our people properly, Laura. My father always taught me that if you look after your workers, they'll look after you. I've lived by that ethic and it's always served me well."

"That's very commendable, JJ, I would guess that there are very few companies that could say the same thing. How have you managed to make this work for you?"

"Oh, that's quite simple" replied JJ with a twinkle in his eye. "Come with me."

JJ took Laura back into the factory, and tapped one of the ladies working on the production line on the shoulder.

"Melanie, this is Laura – she's joining us today as one of our new Brand Managers."

The two women exchanged pleasantries.

"Now, Mel, how many holiday days do you get a year?," asked JJ looking at Laura with a 'wait 'til you hear this' look in his eye.

Melanie laughed. "As many as I like, JJ" she replied.

Laura looked confused. "What do you mean as many as you like?"

"Well, I've been working for a while, so I know what's 'normal' in terms of holidays, but at Gabriels there's no set

❝ ...*in low trust groups, interpersonal relationships interfere with and distort perceptions of the problem.*

Energy and creativity are diverted from finding comprehensive, realistic solutions, and members use the problem as an instrument to minimise their vulnerability.

In contrast, in high trust groups there is less socially generated uncertainty and problems are solved more effectively. **❞**

Zand (1972)

holiday allowance as such. You just take what you need. I took 20 days last year, but I took 29 the year before because I went to Australia to see my sister get married. It's up to you, but I would never abuse the trust that JJ places in me – I love working here too much to jeopardise that."

JJ and Melanie looked at each other and smiled.

"So, what you're saying is you just police yourself – you decide how much holiday you need, and you are trusted to take that time off."

"Yup."

Laura was stunned. She had never heard of anything like this before.

"And Mel," continued JJ, "tell Laura about your working hours."

Mel smiled. "Oh, yes, right – well I don't have set working hours either."

By this stage, Laura was looking flummoxed.

JJ picked up where Melanie had left off. "The idea is that we have a target for production each day, and the staff organise themselves to make sure it is achieved. In fact, most days they produce on average 10% more than they need to because they are 'in the rhythm' and they almost forget to stop! So, if people are 'morning' people, they tend to come in really early; if someone has had a late night, they can sleep in a little and join the team later. Those who are working parents have the flexibility to come in after they've dropped the kids off, and then they usually pop in after the kids have gone to bed, or sometimes for a few hours on a weekend, to make sure that any odd jobs

Psychological contract

In addition to the explicit employment contract, people also create an implicit interpretation known as a 'psychological contract', consisting of the mutual expectations of both the employer and employee. Acceptance of the psychological contract shapes employees' behaviour as they weigh up their obligations towards the organisation, against the organisation's obligations towards them (entitlements), and adjust their behaviour according to whether obligations have been met.

Research shows that companies that treat people as an asset have more success. Such so-called high-performance organisations are characterised by the following:
- Employees are involved and committed
- Employees take responsibility
- Employees have a say in how their work is to be done
- Employees are encouraged to build new skills and competencies
- Employees are given opportunity to use what they have learned and are rewarded for it

are finished off."

Laura was silent. "How do you monitor those people that aren't pulling their weight? How do you manage that?."

"Ah, well, that's where it gets clever" replied JJ. "If someone isn't pulling their weight their colleagues usually figure that out for themselves, and they will sit down with their colleague and point that out. I rarely have to get involved. They operate like a little family. If one of the family is straying, they reel them back in themselves and get them back on the straight and narrow."

"I studied business at university for three years, and I have never heard of any business running itself like this!" exclaimed Laura. "How do you manage to sustain this? How does it work?" There was a hint of exasperation in her voice.

JJ put a reassuring arm around Laura's shoulders.

"Now this is the clever bit. It's simple! I treat people like people. I believe that the vast majority of people are trustworthy and can make decisions for themselves. In fact, the more rules and regulations that you give people as a structure for their working lives, the more that you restrict them. I believe that if you give them the space and span of control to make their own decisions about their working patterns, then you will rarely be disappointed. And, you know what, so far that has served me extremely well."

"Thanks, Melanie." JJ winked at Mel and led Laura away as Mel turned her attention back to the production line.

"Business is all about relationships, Laura. Heck, life is all about relationships." Laura nodded in agreement.

Advocates of relational marketing argue that the likelihood that customers will switch to competitors is significantly reduced when companies implement marketing strategies that maintain and develop close customer relationships.

Customer focussed cues which can lead to trust include:

- Availability or familiarity - frequent exposure to a brand or company
- Appearance – attractive packaging or general ambience of shops/offices, designed to match the desired market (for example, cheap 'n' cheerful, expensive and unique)
- Popularity – visible evidence of a fast turnover of goods indicates a popular product
- A 'caring' company – helpful staff, a good returns policy, loyalty cards, caring employment policies (e.g. employing older or disabled persons), advertising images, courtesy calls, public demonstrations of a caring senior management.

JJ continued. "And trust is at the heart of those relationships. If you give people your trust, you will rarely be disappointed. It's such a precious commodity." Laura could tell that JJ was sincere – it was obvious that this was very important to him. She listened intently as he continued.

"I've certainly been rewarded by keeping that philosophy at the centre of all aspects of my life – work included. Trust is the most fundamental element in business. How can you have any form of a meaningful relationship with people without there being trust between you?"

66 *Trust is cheaper than lawyers* **99**

Charles Handy, writer

Laura settled into Gabriels well. Her role as a Brand Manager took her all over the organisation, and she quickly got to know people. She took JJ's advice to heart and made sure that she formed relationships with those people whom she would come to rely on. And rely on them she did. When she had a request from a customer that meant she had to provide him with a large delivery the following day, having taken the time to get to know Harry, the Despatch Manager, proved a good investment. When one of her customers asked for an outsize version of one of Gabriels most famous products, Chocobubble, for a promotion to tie in with a local event, Laura was able to persuade Kevin in Production to set up a production line especially to satisfy Laura's request. As a result of these and many other relationships which gave Laura the edge when looking after her customers, Laura Anderson quickly developed a strong reputation, both within Gabriels as a customer focused go-getter, and also amongst her customers as someone who would break the rules to make sure that they got the very best service.

The net result was that Laura progressed steadily and quickly up the career ladder at Gabriels. She was nominated for 'Employee of the Month' no less than six times in 18

Relational Trust

Organisations have come to realise how much influence interpersonal relationships have on the way that they function and trust is essential to the development of these relationships.

Some research suggests that there are two forms of trust, situational and relational.

Situational trust is based on one person's perception of the other's competence to fulfil a particular role or task. It develops in an impersonal, objective way, devoid of any emotional attachment. Competence based trust can emerge quickly since it doesn't require development of a personal relationship.

Relational trust focuses on judgements about an individual's personal motives. It takes longer to develop because both parties must be able to read each other's intentions accurately. Breakdowns in motive-based trust are much harder to forgive and give rise to extreme emotions, often carrying greater negative relationship impact than breaches of competence based trust.

Atkinson, S. & Butcher, D. General Management Development Group, Cranfield School of Management
www.cranfield.ac.uk/som/gmdp

months, and 'Employee of the Quarter' twice within the same period. This unprecedented success brought with it more responsibility, greater opportunities to showcase her achievement and, in time, increased access to the senior executives at Gabriels, including JJ. Laura initially found this exposure daunting, but quickly discovered that she enjoyed the increased status that her achievement had brought her. In fact, she soon realised that she enjoyed it very much.

Increasingly, she began to enjoy it a little too much.

❝ A man who doesn't trust himself can never really trust anyone else ❞

Cardinal De Retz

"What do you mean, No?" asked Laura, just shy of shouting.

"Well, it just can't be done that quickly – we're flat out as we are" explained Kevin, the Production Manager. Kevin had been with Gabriels for 14 years – he had started as an apprentice and worked his way up from there. He was very good at his job – he knew the production capacities of his production lines like the back of his hand. Like most people that worked at Gabriels, Kevin valued the relationships that he had with his co-workers – many had become good friends and in many ways Gabriels was more like a family. In fact, he saw his Gabriels 'family' more than he saw his real one. He didn't like it when there was bad feeling with someone at work.

And he certainly wasn't feeling any love from Laura.

"I don't think you understand, Kevin. This is for Jackmans, you know, the biggest supermarket chain in the country" she said sarcastically. "Whatever they want, they get. They need this order, and they need it now. I've promised it to them."

"I'm sorry, Laura, really I am – but we're flat out today. All of this," he gestured to the production line spitting out line after line of chocolate bars at incredible speed "is promised to another company – I can't get you a production slot

10 Principles for Being a Trustworthy Person

1. Because trust is based on truth, trustworthy people must be truthful

2. Trustworthy people are honest

3. Trustworthy people are reliable; they keep their promises

4. Trustworthy people are loyal

5. Trustworthy people are not biased or predjudiced

6. Trustworthy people are humble, recognising that the truth may not always be with them

7. Trustworthy people are accountable

8. Trustworthy people are cooperative

9. Trustworthy people are just

10. Trustworthy people promote communication and understanding

Carl A. Osborne, www.dvmnews.com

until next Tuesday." Kevin was sincere, he would help if he could. He was one of those people that hated to let anyone down.

"You don't know who you're dealing with here, Kevin. You'll regret this." Laura spat her words out at Kevin and, before he could even respond, she had turned on her heels and stomped away.

Kevin turned back toward the production line looking dejected, and shook his head in disbelief.

66 *A competitive culture endures by tearing people down.* **99**

Jules Henry, Anthropologist

Laura muttered to herself under her breath as she walked through Despatch back towards the executive offices. Either side of her were pallets of various products, all stacked and sealed and ready for distribution. As she walked past the pallets, stacked one on top of each other and towering above her, something caught her eye. She stopped and looked more closely. She had thought she spotted the familiar logo out of the corner of her eye. She was right – the brown and gold logo was recognisable anywhere. Four pallets, stacked high with boxes of Dairy Gold – two hundred boxes per pallet to be precise. Together, the four pallets were exactly what Laura had promised to Jackmans, and what Kevin couldn't produce for her in time. Laura walked around the pallets looking for a delivery address – who were these set aside for? she wondered. The pallets were loosely tied together with twine, keeping them together to make sure that they were delivered as one. Laura traced the twine around the pallets until she found what she was looking for: an A4 piece of a paper with the delivery address scribbled in black marker pen: World Foods Mart, Oxford.

Laura opened up the leather folder that she carried everywhere with her and ripped off a sheet of paper from the pad. After taking the pen from the little loop of leather

Dasani Debacle

In 2004, in an attempt to offer a healthier alternative to sugary soda, Coca-Cola entered the lucrative UK bottled water market, a sector dominated by products derived from volcanic springs and mountain streams. Dasani purified water was backed by a multi-million pound launch. Just two weeks after launch, impurities were found in the product leading to total product recall.

The situation worsened as editorial coverage revealed that the source of the water was not a mountain spring as many consumers had assumed, but the same water supplied to homes across the South of England by Thames Water. Coca-Cola were simply bottling tap water, albeit after passing it through a purification process.

Although no one was harmed by the impurities, Dasani's reputation in the UK was damaged beyond repair and, despite Dasani being one of Coca-Cola's leading brands around the globe, it has never been relaunched in the UK.

in the crease of her folder, she turned the paper landscape, leant on the pallet of Dairy Gold in front of her, and wrote JACKMAN'S HILLINGBOROUGH in large capital letters. Then, after stopping to look behind her to make sure that she wasn't seen, she ripped off the piece of paper that hung from the twine and replaced it with the one that she had just written.

Laura snuck the original delivery note into her leather folder and continued on her journey towards the executive offices, a smug smile on her face.

" To be honest is to be real, genuine, authentic, and bona fide. To be dishonest is to be partly feigned, forged, fake, or fictitious. Honesty expresses both self-respect and respect for others. Dishonesty fully respects neither oneself nor others. Honesty imbues lives with openness, reliability, and candor; it expresses a disposition to live in the light. Dishonesty seeks shade, cover, or concealment. It is a disposition to live partly in the dark. "

William J. Bennett, The Book of Virtues

"Nice motor, Jeremy!" shouted Laura from across the car park. She had noticed that her colleague had a new car. A brand new BMW, no less. Sleek and silver, it was quite an eye catcher.

"Have you opted out of the company car scheme then?" asked Laura, in as nonchalant a manner as she could muster. She had always wanted a BMW – it was one of the goals that she had set herself. In Laura's mind she would know when she had 'made it' - when she was behind the wheel of a brand new Beamer.

"Oh no, this is a company car – I've just changed mine."

"Awesome – are BMWs on the list now? My Ford is up for renewal soon – I might get myself one of those beauties."

Jeremy looked sheepish. "Oh, the BMW's not on the list, Laura – I was lucky to get this."

"Well, how did you manage to get it if it's not on the list? Peter Taylor manages the company car budget as if it was his own money. How did you wangle that?" said Laura laughing, trying not to let her envy show.

"I've got back problems, and my old car didn't give me the support that I needed. The seat in the BMW is so much better than the car grade that I was entitled to and there was a price difference that Peter could live with, so he signed it off. I think he was secretly worried about what

Office Politics

In a study published in 2003, researchers investigated the concepts of lies and organisational politics in an attempt to compare the similarities and differences and identify the pitfalls of an organisation suffering from a politically charged climate.

The main similarity between the concept of lying and organisational politics is that the advantage of deception in both cases helps to maintain relationships within the organisation on a short-term basis. When deception is discovered, however, trust and co-operation are adversely affected.

Organisational politics encompasses a wider range of behaviours and is a more complex concept with multifaceted consequences. A politically charged organisation faces reduced job satisfaction, increased anxiety and stress, increased turnover and reduced performance. To overturn these outcomes a manager must lead with integrity and promote a climate of trust.

Curtis, S. (2003). Lies, damned lies and organisational politics.
Industrial and Commercial Training. 35 (7). 293-297.

would happen if my back got worse and I ended up taking some time off sick. He knew that JJ wouldn't be happy about that, so he ok'd it."

"Did he now?" came the curt reply.

66 *The opposite of integrity is manipulation* **99**

Thesaurus

Whilst she sat at the lights waiting for them to turn green, Laura stroked the leather steering wheel of her brand new car. Whilst he didn't quite stretch to leather seats, Laura was delighted with what she had managed to wangle out of Peter Taylor. What's good for the goose is good for the gander, she had thought to herself as she approached Peter in his office a short time after her conversation with Jeremy in the Gabriels staff car park.

Peter had initially declined outright Laura's suggestion that she needed an upgrade to a BMW. Despite her protestations that she needed to take clients out on occasion and that a BMW created a much more professional impression, and that the Beamer would be a better investment for the company in the long run, he had made it clear that the exception that he had made for Jeremy was precisely that. An exception.

" IT'S PROBABLY JUST SOMETHING
YOU PICKED UP AT THE OFFICE "

Laura didn't really regret lying to Peter that she also suffered from back pain and needed more support for the long journeys up and down the motorway. Nor did she regret suggesting to Peter that he was discriminating against her by upgrading a male colleague, but not her. She didn't even regret implying that a sex discrimination lawsuit would sting Gabriels for more than the cost of the BMW.

Now that she was sitting behind the wheel of her new BMW, Laura didn't regret a thing.

❝ *I've learned that it takes years to build up trust and it only takes suspicion, not proof, to destroy it in an instant.* **❞**

Anon

"It's beautiful" said Laura in awe.

The sales assistant stood silently while Laura examined the bag. A deep brown, made from the softest calf leather and with a huge flamboyant, yet feminine, buckle on the front, the bag was certainly something special. And at just under four figures, it would need to be.

"It really suits you" said the sales assistant softly. She knew that the bag sold itself, and she could also see that Laura had already made her mind up. She waited patiently whilst her customer examined every inch of the bag.

After a short while, Laura turned to the assistant with a smile on her face. She looked like the cat that got the cream.

"You know what, I deserve a treat - I've had a really good month, blown my targets. Why not, I'll take it!"

The assistant smiled and floated off towards the cash desk.

"The girls at work will be so jealous" said Laura whilst she watched her extravagant new purchase being wrapped in tissue paper.

66 *When people honor each other, there is a trust established that leads to synergy, interdependence, and deep respect. Both parties make decisions and choices based on what is right, what is best, what is valued most highly.* **99**

Blaine Lee, author of The Power Principle

"You've spent how much?"

Tom was doing his best not to lose his temper with his girlfriend.

"It doesn't matter how much it cost, Tom, I deserve it, I've had a really good month."

"I know you have – and I thought that the proceeds of your really good month were going into our wedding fund, Laura."

"Well, I just thought I deserved a treat."

"Deserved a treat? Deserved a treat? I have been working extra shifts for the last few months and taking a packed lunch to the fire station every day to scrimp every penny together to give you the wedding that you want. I've even passed on my season ticket at the footie this season to save some more cash. And you go and blow all that money on a bloody handbag! Are you insane?"

Laura had never seen Tom like this before. Never. He was usually so level-headed and straight down the line. The couple were the envy of all their friends as they never argued, and she had certainly never seen him lose his temper like this before. He was obviously very upset.

"I'm sorry, darling, I couldn't resist it – it's the 'in' bag right now, there's even a waiting list for them. I'm lucky to get one." Laura regretted saying that the moment the

Money's too tight to mention

Debt and finance are significant factors in the breakdown of marriage and co-habiting relationships. Relate, the relationship guidance organisation, report that over 44% of couples argue over the issue of finance.

A common problem is that individuals hide their debt problem from their partner, leading to a breakdown of trust within the relationship on top of a mounting financial strain.

words had fallen from her lips.

Tom looked at her aghast. "Lucky to get one?"

"At the end of the day, it's my money and I'll do what I want with it" said Laura impertinently.

That was it. Laura had gone too far. Tom looked at his girlfriend with a combination of sadness and pity in his eyes. The two stood in silence for a moment that seemed to last forever.

❝ *Leadership is not about demanding trust and respect. It's about giving trust and respect* **❞**

Lord Bilimora, Founder Cobra Beer

Approached by JJ one day while she was preparing a presentation pitch to win a new account, Laura's big break came out of the blue.

"Laura, I think it's about time we put your strategic creativity to the test. There's a lot of talk of the importance of Fairtrade in the chocolate industry, and we don't have any ethically traded chocolates or confectionery products in our portfolio. I'd like you to investigate getting a Gabriels fairly traded product onto the shelves."

"Sure thing, JJ – leave it to me."

"I have a Board meeting a week today and I'd like you to present this then – the sooner the better."

JJ knew that was an unbelievably tight deadline, as did Laura. But there was no way that she was going to let that distract her. This was a project for JJ, and one that also presented her with an opportunity to present to the Board. She wasn't going to let this golden opportunity pass her by.

66 *Leadership is a position of trust and in any position of trust the greater burden of responsibility rests on the party that has the most power.* **99**

Tom Marshall, author *Understanding Leadership*

Laura spent the next week scurrying around gathering information and ideas wherever she could find them. She trawled around the local stores buying every example of Fairtrade chocolate that she could find.

She spent time with the Buyers and the Research & Development people in the kitchens, and spent hours at home every evening trawling the internet for nuggets of information. She was determined that she was going to make the most of this opportunity and create a proposal for JJ that was so compelling that he couldn't possibly turn it down.

However, the reality wasn't that simple. Without exception, every person that she spoke to whilst piecing together her little jigsaw gave her the same insight: creating a reasonably priced, competitive, ethical chocolate bar was well nigh impossible. In fact, over the last few years, it had become known as the Holy Grail of the chocolate industry.

Laura, however, simply wasn't prepared to accept that it couldn't be done. She reviewed her research and notes again and again.

Boss's Privilege led to Prison

Conrad Black was convicted on July 13th 2007 on multiple counts of fraud making him one of the most famous casualties of modern day greed and corruption. The BBC reported at the time:

"Black, who remained impassive as the verdicts were read out, was found guilty of taking money owed to the investors in the form of 'non-compete' payments originating from the sale of newspaper titles."

In sentencing Black to federal prison, Judge Amy St. Eve told him "Corporate executives have a duty to act in shareholders' best interests – not in their selfish interests," and that he had abused the trust of his shareholders. "I cannot understand how somebody of your stature could engage in the conduct you engaged in and put everything at risk."

In the small hours of the morning, and with her big presentation mere hours away, Laura finally found a loophole. She had come up with a cunning plan, a way of delivering to JJ exactly what he desired.

*" A pocketful of mumbles, such are promises.
All lies and jests – still a man hears what he wants to hear and disregards the rest… "*

Paul Simon, "The Boxer"

Laura made sure that she was at the Boardroom in plenty of time. Dressed in a new suit which she had bought especially for the occasion, her expensive new handbag was the perfect accessory. She looked smart, she looked confident, she looked professional.

Laura was surprised at the warmth of the welcome that she received from the Board. JJ had clearly briefed them on the challenge that he had set for his young protégée and, as a result, the Board were eager to hear Laura's proposals. Was Laura about to solve the challenge that had eluded the confectionery business for the past few years? Judging from the first few slides and Laura's confident delivery, it appeared that she was.

That was until, halfway through her PowerPoint deck, and in the midst of describing the cunning plan to succeed where the rest of the industry had failed, JJ interrupted.

"So, Laura, what are you saying? Are you saying that the chocolate that we use for this bar is not actually ethically traded?" JJ couldn't quite believe what he had just heard. The other members of the Board stopped fiddling with their pens and their mobile phones and fixed their focus on JJ.

The Fairtrade Mark

The Fairtrade Foundation was established in 1992 and is the UK member of Fairtrade Labelling Organisations International.

The FAIRTRADE Mark is a certification label awarded to products sourced from the developing world that meet internationally recognised standards of fair trade.

Trading standards stipulate that traders must:
- Pay a price to producers that covers the costs of sustainable production and living
- Pay a premium that producers can invest in development
- Make partial advance payments when requested by producers
- Sign contracts that allow for long-term planning and sustainable production practices

Currently more than 900 retail and catering products from coffee to wine carry the FAIRTRADE mark in the UK and retail sales of these products are increasing by over 40% each year. In 2007, the world wide retail value of these products was approx. 2 billion Euros.

www.fairtrade.net

His eye contact, however, was fixed squarely on Laura.

"Well, it's almost ethical" stuttered Laura, shifting her weight from one foot to the other.

"Almost ethical? Almost ethical? What does almost ethical mean exactly, Laura, eh?" In an instant, the atmosphere in the room changed. Everyone, including Laura, was dumbstruck at JJ's reaction. The playful maverick had been replaced by a fierce and focused businessman who clearly wasn't happy with what he was hearing.

JJ took another breath to continue. Laura braced herself.

"Does it mean that you'll pay the farmers a slightly better price than they get from the big time corporate cowboys? Or perhaps you're going to make sure that the minimum age of the children who work like slaves for the growers is capped at nine, rather than the seven year olds that are currently sent out to the fields in lieu of any education? Is that it, Laura? Please do tell me what almost ethical means – I'd love to know." JJ angrily swept his arm in front of the Board sitting around the long oak table. "I'm sure we're *all* intrigued by your definition."

JJ hadn't broken his eye contact with Laura once. She wasn't sure if he had even blinked since he started ranting at her.

"Well, um, it's more a case of, er, well it's just being economical with the truth a little, you know, er, well, no-one will ever know…"

JJ let out a little snort.

"No-one will ever know? Listen to yourself! This is ridiculous. In fact it's more than ridiculous, it's offensive,

Corporate Social Responsibility in Brands

As the population becomes more media savvy, companies need to adopt new techniques for integrating CSR into brands. Examples:

1. Traceability – acknowledge the source of materials and completely trace the process through manufacture and distribution to give clear indication of how products reach the shelves.

2. Flexible working – companies who adopt adaptive working conditions and openly trust their employees to deliver are viewed more favourably than those who install inflexible conditions.

3. Depth in Marketing – increasingly consumers are interested in knowing about the story behind the product.

4. Word of mouth – CSR is best communicated locally and informally through staff who are highly interactive with their customers.

5. Vision – be proactive not reactive. Don't be afraid to set industry standards and keep moving above and beyond them to stay ahead.

and it's disrespectful. Disrespectful to me, to my Board, to my family who have built this company from nothing to greatness, but most of all it's disrespectful to our customers. Customers who have believed in Gabriels for generations."

JJ paused again and Laura stood, embarrassed, at the front of the room. The Board all stared at Laura, all with a look of incredulation, some shaking their heads in disbelief.

"Get out."

Laura was jolted from the coma of guilt at the front of the room. "I'm sorry?"

"Are you? I'm not sure. But I'll tell you what I am sure of, Laura. There is no room in Gabriels for liars, nor for people who undermine the very fabric of our company. There's no room here for people who set out to deceive or disrespect our customers. You have achieved all of those things in your presentation today."

"Perhaps we could talk about this later?" Laura looked to JJ with a nervous smile on her face.

"There will be no later, Laura. I want you to clear your desk, and leave your car keys at reception. Your career at Gabriels is over."

JJ stared at Laura as the implications of his words hit her. And they hit her hard. As she collected together her papers, her eyes welled up, and within moments she was crying. Crying at the front of the Boardroom. In front of the Board. With no job. No respect. Her career, her reputation, in shreds.

The Board all filed out of the Boardroom, leaving her to

Supermarkets do the right thing

The Co-operative chain of stores in the UK was the first to commit that all own brand products would be sourced from Fairtrade suppliers. Some years later, the UK's second largest food retailer, Sainsbury's, were also the first UK retailer to convert its entire banana range to 100% Fairtrade. Selling over a thousand bananas each minute, the move has made a significant difference to hundreds of farmers, with £4 million of social premium generated in 2007 alone. They also ordered 40 tonnes of Fairtrade cocoa to produce over eight million chocolate squares to include in 2007's Comic Relief campaign.

gather together her presentation. The heavy door closed behind them and she was left in the imposing room on her own. Just 30 minutes ago she had entered the room positive and enthusiastic about her project. What a difference 30 minutes make. With tears streaming down her face, she turned towards the floor to ceiling window and looked down at the bustling factory below her.

Her moment of reflection was interrupted as one of the tea ladies came into the Boardroom with her trolley to clear away the tea and biscuits.

"Oh, sorry love, I didn't know there was anyone left in here. You finished?"

"Yes" replied Laura thoughtfully. "I think I probably am."

66 *We need people in our lives with whom we can be as open as possible. To have real conversation with people may seem like such a simple, obvious suggestion, but it involves courage and risk.* 99

Thomas Moore, Irish Poet

The journey home was not a pleasant one. The repercussions of what she had just done slowly began to dawn on Laura. She would have to tell her parents, so proud of her for rising to such a prestigious role within Gabriels, a company which meant so much to their family, that she had been fired. She would have to tell Tom. She would have to find another job, and quickly. But who would take her on when they found out the real reason for her leaving Gabriels? Laura was despondent.

Laura's thought pattern was interrupted by the loud rumble of a bus behind her. As she happened to be walking past a bus stop at that very moment, she stuck out her arm and the bus pulled up alongside her.

"Where to darlin'?" asked the bus driver smiling.

"Erm, I'm not sure" said Laura feeling out of her depth – it had been quite some time since she had travelled on public transport. She grappled with her handbag, and fumbled around for her purse, beginning to sense that most of the other passengers were now staring at her with a mixture of disbelief and frustration that her apparent dithering was keeping them all waiting.

"Do you go anywhere near Dahomey Road?"

"We go down the High Street, which is just round the

Mistakes

The key to creative, happy and motivated staff is the freedom to make mistakes and learn from them. You can only learn from a mistake once you have admitted (even just to yourself) that a mistake has been made. Admission of a mistake makes learning possible by moving the focus away from blame assignment and towards understanding. Learning from mistakes requires three things:

- Putting yourself in situations where you can make interesting mistakes
- Having the self-confidence to admit to them
- Being courageous about making changes

corner, sweetheart, that do you?" he asked, clearly seeing that Laura wasn't a regular bus traveller.

Laura smiled. "That's fine, thank you."

Laura made her way down the bus, reaching for the handrail to steady herself as the bus lurched away from the bus stop. She flopped down into a seat next to an older lady, and put her purse away. When she had settled herself, she looked to her left and smiled at the old lady who had moved her bag so that Laura could take the empty seat. The old lady responded accordingly.

"Don't you get the bus very often then, dear?" asked the old lady.

Sensing that she wanted some conversation, Laura obliged.

"No, not that often" she said. "I usually drive everywhere," and with that her bottom lip began to quiver.

"Oh, sorry, my love, I didn't mean to upset you."

Laura turned and smiled, wiping away the tears with her forefingers. "I'm ok, it's fine, thank you, really, I'm fine."

"Yes, us girls have a habit of saying "I'm fine" when really that couldn't be further from the truth!" she added, with more than a hint of playful sarcasm in her voice. "And usually, there's a man involved!" she continued, nudging Laura playfully.

Laura smirked. "Yes, there is a man involved as it happens…" and before she could continue, her new friend stopped Laura in her tracks.

"I knew it!" came the triumphant reply. "So, come on, let's have it, what's he done?"

A problem shared is a problem halved

During times of anguish it is often easier to share our concerns with a stranger than a friend. In the UK and Ireland the Samaritans provided telephone support to nearly 5 million anonymous callers, emailers and branch visitors in despair during 2007.

The rise of internet chat rooms, counselling and coaching indicates a growing willingness to trust a stranger with our concerns ahead of friends and family.

To be an effective trusted stranger or indeed friend we must be able to demonstrate 'empathy'. Defined by Wittig and Belkin in 1990 as;

"The quality of feeling as another feels, to experience another's reality from that person's point of view."

"Well, it's quite complicated, but basically he fired me. But it's all my own fault."

"Oh dear. Well that's not what I expected you to say" replied the old lady, slightly embarrassed.

"When I left the house this morning, I didn't expect to be sitting on a bus in the afternoon, having been fired by JJ Gabriel."

"Fired by JJ? Goodness me, however did you manage that? He's meant to be such a lovely man, and so good to his staff. You must have done something really bad for him to take such a drastic course of action."

"Well, yes, I suppose I did. With hindsight I can't quite believe that I did it, to be honest."

"And what is 'it', dear? What did you do exactly?" she asked, with apprehension clear in her voice at what this young woman was about to disclose.

Laura sighed, as if to centre herself. "I look after..." she paused. "Sorry, I used to look after some products at Gabriels, and I suggested that we launch a new product and be economical with the truth about the source of the product."

"You mean to lie?" asked the old lady, with a disapproving air.

Laura sighed again. "Yes."

"Well, I can see why he fired you." she said, deadpan, shuffling in her seat.

Laura was taken aback by the response. She had been so friendly and understanding up until this point. Clearly she wasn't impressed either. Laura's feeling of guilt, which

"Tell them I'm not here"

In his book 'Thank God It's Monday', Mark Greene tells a story of an experienced secretary who takes a job as personal assistant to a high ranking military leader. On the first day she was putting a call through to her new boss from a particularly demanding individual. On hearing who was on the line, the respected leader asked his new PA to tell the caller he was out, as do so many managers every day.

"I can't do that, you are here" came the response from the new secretary.

After a pause she continued, "If I lie *for* you now, you won't know when I'm lying *to* you."

had slightly dissipated whilst she was speaking to her new found friend, resurged with a vengeance.

The two sat in silence. Clearly what Laura had disclosed had killed the conversation stone dead.

The bus continued on its journey, with people bustling past Laura at every stop to go about their business.

"I lied once" came the soft voice from beside her. In fact it was so soft that Laura couldn't be sure that she actually heard it correctly. She turned to look at the old woman who was gazing out of the window, apparently misty eyed.

"Sorry, did you say something?" asked Laura.

Turning to face her, her eyes belied the fact that she had been crying.

"Whatever's the matter?" Laura asked with genuine concern.

"I lied once" repeated the woman.

"It cost me my happiness, my future, my life" she continued, her voice drifting to a whisper as she spoke.

Laura was dumbstruck. This woman, who had been so sweet and unassuming, was now contemplative, and more than a little upset.

"I'm sorry – I didn't mean to burden you with my problems. I certainly didn't want to upset you. I'm so sorry."

She patted Laura on the arm, and smiled meekly.

"It's fine, dear, you just brought back some memories that I would rather forget, that's all."

The two women exchanged a warm hearted glance. The old lady shuffled in her seat so as to move her body to face

Traders' lies generate £100 million profit

One Wednesday in March 2008 shares in the fifth largest UK bank, HBOS, fell by 17% in the first hour of trading. All as a result of untrue rumours of a liquidity crisis at HBOS circulating London trading floors by email.

It is widely believed that these emails were created by an opportunist trader who may well have achieved £100 million profit on the shares' rapid descent in value and subsequent rise to normal levels within a matter of days.

Laura, and took a deep breath as if to brace herself. Laura sensed that she was about to hear something important.

"It was a long time ago, but you know, it has haunted me ever since."

Despite her embarrassment that she had quite unintentionally upset a random person on the bus, Laura felt compelled to listen.

"I made a huge mistake, my dear, when I wasn't much older than you are now. I told a single, dreadful lie that, with hindsight, ended costing me my happiness. I was never able to repair the damage of that lie. Not a day goes by when I don't pine for what could have been and wish I could turn the clock back."

She fixed Laura with an intense stare and took her young friend's hand in hers. She patted it softly as she spoke.

"Make amends, my dear. Don't let your lie consume your life the way that it has consumed mine."

Just as she turned towards the window, Laura saw that the old lady had tears welling in her eyes.

This woman's lie had affected her whole life. Was that to be Laura's destiny? As she contemplated this possibility, she became overcome with a feeling of despair.

66 *Truthfulness builds trust: lies destroy it* **99**

Anon

Just as soon as Laura had arrived home, she dropped her bag onto the floor, peeled off her suit jacket, kicked off her shoes and flopped onto the sofa. She sighed deeply as she relaxed into the soft sofa cushions. Staring at the ceiling as her thoughts drifted, she considered the day.

She had left the flat that morning so enthusiastic and confident – her big chance to shine in front of the Board. Instead, here she was, lying on the sofa in the middle of the afternoon with no job, no car, and very little dignity. It hadn't been a good day. Laura groaned and pushed her face into the cushions of the sofa as it dawned on her that she had yet to tell Tom what had happened. That wasn't going to be a great conversation. Tom was already on a downer with her. What on earth was she doing? Not so long ago she had a loving relationship with a boyfriend she adored, and a job that she loved and where she was rising fast up the corporate ladder, with all the trappings of success that came with it. She was the envy of all her friends, and the source of a great deal of pride for her parents.
Now look at me, she thought. What have I done?

Laura glanced at her watch – four o'clock. Tom would be getting home soon. She reluctantly dragged herself from

Time to Think

Many argue that there's no time to stop and reflect in the modern world, as constant telephone calls and a continuous stream of emails occupy every waking thought. Those moments of inspiration made famous by Sir Issac Newton's time thinking in the orchard are hard to find these days. Arthur Fry famously invented the Post-it note in a church, not in a 3M laboratory.

Allan Leighton, the extraordinary business leader who has held top positions at ASDA, Royal Mail, Bhs and Loblaw Cos, often at the same time, spends forty minutes every day running and reckons; "Taking forty minutes a day just thinking saves forty days of chaos."

So when thinking time is forced upon us either by a change of role or a delayed flight, we should see it as an opportunity for our next 'Eureka!' moment.

the sofa and went to the kitchen, checking out the contents of the fridge. She had been so focused on preparing her presentation over the last few days that she hadn't been to a supermarket and there was a pretty poor and eclectic selection of food left in the fridge.

Laura sighed. "Not much I can do with this" she murmured, rifling through the contents of the fridge.

Laura retrieved her shoes and her handbag and made for the door.

66 *Surveys of happiness reveal that there is no relationship between level of income and general satisfaction with one's life.* **99**

David Myers, author, *In Pursuit of Happiness*

The High Street was busy with people milling around. It was so long since Laura had been out shopping during the week that she had quite forgotten that the people who she saw out shopping on a Saturday were quite different from those who populated the High Street during the week. Used to yuppie couples and young families, Laura instead found herself negotiating old people and mums with pushchairs as she wandered down the High Street looking for somewhere suitable to buy something for dinner. During her short walk from the flat, Laura had decided that she would try and do some damage limitation with Tom by cooking a nice meal. Since their holiday in Italy a year or so ago, Tom had become a real fan of Italian food, so Laura had decided that she should employ the old adage 'the way to a man's heart is through his stomach' and cook him something hearty and Italian, in the hope that he wouldn't completely blow his stack when she recounted her disastrous day to him.

Laura was considering the options of where best to buy her ingredients when she was handed a flyer by someone distributing leaflets in the street. Laura took a look as she was walking. Perfect! Unbeknown to her, a new deli had just opened up in one of the side roads off the High Street, just a few minutes walk away. Laura picked up her pace

**64% of employees DISLIKE
what their employer stands for!**

Survey commissioned by Vodafone in 2007

and made her way straight there.

Sure enough, there was the new deli. The town was undergoing some regeneration, and the side street looked like it had recently had a significant amount of love and attention from the town planners. The concrete had been paved over with cobbles, and the modern street lights had been replaced with some old fashioned alternatives which, being much more attractive to look at and shorter than the standard, modern street lights, gave the street quite a different, more sophisticated feel from the main High Street. The bunting that had been hung the length of the short street from the street lights made the little street feel cosy and welcoming. The shop fascias had been redeveloped to reflect the yesteryear feel, and the deli on the right-hand side had been painted a deep blue. The gold lettering simply spelling out the word DELICATESSEN above the window completed the stylish feel of Victoriana.

'Wow, this is great" muttered Laura to herself. This was quite a find.

Laura made her way inside the shop, past the couple of little café tables and chairs that were positioned outside on the pavement. The old-fashioned feel had been continued inside: bare floorboards, with a little sawdust scattered on the floor to give an authentic traditional feel. The shop smelt amazing. Huge hams hung from hooks on the low ceiling, enormous round cheeses sat on the counter, and light wooden shelves were stacked full of European looking tins, bottles and jars: a foodie's treasure trove. Laura drew

Blue is cited as the best colour for brand building and is associated with trust and credibility according to research by The Future Laboratory

a deep breath – the air tasted delicious! For a split second, her troubles seemed far behind her.

"Laura!"

The man, wearing a white apron and carrying a huge round of stilton, dropped the huge cheese onto the counter and quickly made his way round the counter into the centre of the shop where Laura was standing, and gave her a kiss on both cheeks.

"Hello darling, how are you? What are you doing here?"

It had all happened so fast Laura was a little overawed, and took a moment to recognise the man.

"Oh my God, Steve, hi, sorry, I was mesmerised by this place, there's so much to take in, sorry, I didn't recognise you. What are you doing here?"

She took a better look at the man in the apron. He was Steve Brown, one of her previous bosses at Gabriels. After years of working in Sales and Marketing for JJ, he had decided that he wanted to run his own business and had left about a year ago. Laura hadn't heard from him since then, and had been too wrapped up in her own career to give him a second thought. It was a pleasant surprise to bump into him, though. Steve had helped Laura when she first joined Gabriels, and had been instrumental in her rising up the ranks as quickly as she had. At the same time as being excited to see him, she felt a twinge of embarrassment that she hadn't kept in touch with him.

"You remember that I left Gabriels with the dream of running something myself?"

"Sure, I remember that – is this it then?"

Listen actively

We can absorb between 600 and 800 words per minute. Listening to someone speaking at a normal pace of somewhere between 100 and 170 words per minute can leave space for our thoughts to wander from what is being said.

By repeating back what has been said to clarify understanding, asking questions and giving feedback, we become an active listener and therefore considerably more likely to be trusted by those speaking to us.

"Certainly is! Well, I wanted to step down a few gears and spend more time with Maria and the boys, so a local business seemed the sensible option. I've always been a foodie – so a top quality delicatessen seemed the perfect choice!"

"Wow – well it's certainly quality – it's gorgeous. Is business good?"

"Very brisk, actually – we've only been open for a few weeks and people are still hearing about us, so I'm sure that we'll do well when the word gets around that we're here. And the streets have been regenerated beautifully, so it couldn't have worked out better really."

"That's great. I'm really pleased for you!" Laura was genuine. She had a lot of time for Steve – he was a good guy, great at his job, and she admired the fact that he had undertaken such a life change so that he could spend more time with his family.

"So, what about you? How are things going at Gabriels?" Laura's smile quickly turned into a frown. "Not great actually, I, I, I've, er..." Laura looked to the floor and her bottom lip began to quiver.

Steve noticed that his friend was becoming upset. "I'll tell you what" he continued in a deliberately upbeat tone, "how about we sit outside and have a coffee, and you can tell me all about it?"

Laura smiled, and wiped a tear from her eye. "That would be great, thanks."

Steve turned to the young man arranging the meats behind the counter.

Symbols versus Symptoms of trustworthiness

Symbols = learned signifiers of trustworthiness such as kitemarks, ratings, and mission statements.

Symptoms = by-products of trustworthiness such as large numbers of positive customer reviews, repeat business, positive word of mouth stories.

Brand trust, that is the symbols and symptoms of trustworthiness, is individual to each brand so must be explored by marketers and used to build an ongoing relationship with the customer. When advertising online, the focus should be on identifying symptoms and not symbols of trustworthiness, and building upon those.

"William, I'm going to be outside, would you bring us a couple of capps, some of that new delivery of panettone, and keep an eye on the shop for me?"

"Sure thing" came the reply, and Steve led Laura to the café tables outside the shop.

"Here you go, sit yourself down."

Laura proceeded to recount her day, and explain her experience with the Board earlier that morning, stopping only to sip her coffee. Steve sat in silence and listened to his friend's story. When Steve was at Gabriels, he was known as 'Uncle Steve' on account of his ability to listen to the woes of his co-workers and dispense sound advice. He clearly hadn't lost any of those skills. Laura was grateful for having someone to talk to, and she knew that Steve would understand better than anyone.

"Mmmm, sounds like you've got yourself in quite a pickle" said Steve, understating what he had just heard.

Laura smiled. "You could say that. It's all a bit of a mess."

"Yes, you do sound like you've blown it with JJ, rather. Didn't you consider that he might react that way?"

"Well, I was just focused on coming up with the product that he had asked for. It was genuinely difficult to get a fairly traded bar that we could sell at a reasonable price to our customers. And I just figured that they would never know about the pseudo Fairtrade thing. They would just take our word for it."

Steve pointed his finger at Laura. "Aha. That's just it, isn't it?"

"What?"

David beats Goliath in Potato Chip War

In 2002, Will Chase, a Hereford potato farmer turned potato chip maker, set out to make his new brand of Tyrrells Crisps a premium product, available initially only through independent outlets at a premium price. Having suffered at the hands of supermarkets with their aggressive buying and pricing practices during his farming days, he was determined not to have his livelihood threatened in the same way again.

As the brand grew in popularity, Tyrrells was approached by leading UK retailer Tesco. Once bitten, twice shy, Will politely refused their offer to stock his product, opting instead to continue distributing through independent retailers. Tesco refused to take "no" for an answer, and instead sourced Tyrrells on the 'grey market' and, furthermore, listed the product at a discounted price.

Despite requests to Tesco to remove the product in order to protect the brand's Artisan values, Tesco flatly refused. The British media picked up on the story as a national news item, ultimately forcing the retail giant to climb down and discontinue stocking Tyrrells.

Two years on, Tyrrells has continued to go from strength to strength, with export sales into mainland Europe, and over 5,000 outlets stocking the product in the UK, some of which are now supermarkets, although to date always selling at the recommended retail price set by Will and his colleagues back on the farm in Hereford, ensuring that increased popularity won't lead to compromised quality.

"Well, that's what's at the crux of all this – people do take your word for it. People put an immense amount of trust in those who they buy things from – whatever it is. They assume that what they're buying is authentic – that it is what it purports to be. I mean, take me for example, I have some of my cured meats imported from a tiny village in the south of Italy because that's where the best kind of those meats come from. I could go and source something very similar from elsewhere, and my customers would probably never know the difference. But I would. And I couldn't stand behind my counter and tell them that the proscuitto they were buying was from the San Daniele del Friuli region if it really wasn't. And just imagine if a customer somehow found out – they'd think 'well if he's lied about this, what else has he lied about?', and pretty soon I wouldn't have a business left."

Laura nodded. This made sense.

"You know, Laura, I learnt this a long time ago – business isn't about products and services and stuff a lot of the time. It's all about feelings, emotions and relationships. Take you, for example. When I met you in the shop earlier, you were revelling in the smell and the atmosphere that we've created in the shop – your feelings and emotions were taking over your head. How likely was it that you would buy a few bits and pieces?"

"Oh, I was probably going to buy quite a bit, actually."

"Right, absolutely – because the shop and the environment we've created captured your heart."

Laura smiled. "I guess so – I have never thought about it

The Coffee Stain Rule

Our subconscious influences our trust of organisations significantly; dirty surroundings and mess are unlikely to increase our confidence in an organisation's ability to meet our needs.

Every successful airline knows the coffee stain rule. If a passenger finds a coffee stain has not been cleaned on her tray table, she immediately concludes that the engineers may have forgotten to tighten a critical bolt on the airframe. Clean cabins make for calm passengers!

like that."

"What if you then found out that I was pumping in that smell artificially or something? How likely would you be to buy something from me then?"

"Well, I'd feel a bit cheated, so probably not very much, if anything at all in fact."

Steve smiled. "Absolutely. You see, the relationship that I'd created by setting out my shop like that had built a strong bond. A bond of affection. A bond of authenticity. A bond driven by trust."

Steve looked to Laura, who looked like she was giving this some considerable thought.

"Right, so even though I don't see you going to Italy and buying those hams, I trust you that when you say you are getting them from that region in Italy, you really are?"

"Right. And my business rests on that trust. As does JJ's. His business is built on a bond with customers. A bond that means that every time they buy a Gabriels product they will be happy with it – and that trust is integral to his business. He knows that – which is why he was horrified that you were suggesting undermining that. It's almost like an emotional contract between JJ and his customers. And between me and my customers."

"I hadn't thought about it like that. I hadn't considered that emotional contract. I was just focused on the sales and the profits."

Steve laughed. "Yes, there's an echo of 'famous last words' about that statement! Many businesses, huge businesses, have fallen because greed has taken over and trust and

integrity have fallen by the wayside. But it catches up with them. Customers don't like being deceived."

"No, you're right – you know what, I'd lost sight of that. It slipped right off my radar screen."

"Well, let's hope it's back there now, eh?" Steve smiled at Laura. She seemed more than a little happier now than she had been when she walked into his delicatessen that short time ago.

Laura glanced down at her watch. "Oh, my goodness, I didn't realise the time. I have to go!"

"Look, before you go, let me get a little package together for you – a sample of some of our authentic delights," said Steve, winking at Laura. The fact that he had stressed the word authentic hadn't been lost on her.

"That would be wonderful – thanks. I originally came here to get something to cook Tom a nice dinner – he loves Italian."

"Well, I've got the perfect solution" said Steve, striding back into the store, the floorboards creaking underfoot.

He shouted across to William to package up various meats, and duly set to work at the counter. Steve began scooping up delicious looking pasta and sauces from the adjacent counter, and within minutes he presented Laura with a small box of goodies, all neatly packaged and secured with some thick brown twine which captured the essence of the delightfully old-fashioned deli perfectly.

"That looks amazing – thanks Steve. The packaging is beautiful."

"I'm glad you think so – all part of the authenticity.

Emotions in consumerism

Confidence is an essential emotion for consumers, and comes hand in hand with trust. Providing good quality products and services, offering ethical employment policies, affordable pricing and returns policies, and an attractive environment for sales, all contribute to consumer confidence.

National Consumer Council findings show that consumer trust is inspired by: caring policies, evidence of a popular outlet, attractive packaging, and clean, bright and spacious shops. Since most people don't have time to research every purchase they make, consumers also rely heavily on trusted brand symbols which demonstrate that they are approved by regulators.

No point having gorgeous food delivered in a plain old paper bag, is there?"

Laura smiled. "No, I guess you're right."

"Listen – there's somewhere I'd like to take you that will give you some fresh insights into what we've been talking about today. What are you doing on Thursday night?"

"Well, you know, I appear to have a completely free schedule" Laura said with a hint of friendly sarcasm. Steve smiled in response, looking a little embarrassed.

"Ok, well, let's go Thursday. How about I meet you here at seven?"

"Perfect – I'll look forward to it."

"Ok, and good luck for tonight."

"Thanks Steve, I think I might need it. But I have a suspicion that this will help!" Laura lifted the package in the air as she waved goodbye.

66 *Honesty is the best image* **99**

Tom Wilson, Ziggy (comic)

By the time Laura reached the flat, Tom had already been home for some time.

"Hey sweetheart! How did your big presentation go?"

Laura did her very best to sound upbeat and give Tom a warm smile. "Let's talk about that later – look what I got you!" She sang the last few words as she dangled the beautifully wrapped package in front of Tom.

"Wow – looks great – where'd you get that?"

"There's a great new deli that's opened up in Wetherby Street, and I discovered it by accident. It's really lovely, and you remember Steve that used to work with me at Gabriels?"

"Sure – the guy with the baby boys?"

"That's the one – well, you know Steve left a year or so ago? He's opened up this deli, and it's awesome – as good as those little foodie stores that we used to go to when we were on holiday in Italy."

"Ah yes, they were great, weren't they? Well, if Steve's place is as good as they were, then I would imagine we'll become his best customers!"

"Oh, I have a feeling I'll be going back there – it's right up our street, Tom."

"So, what did you get?"

The pair proceeded to open the package, which consisted

The origins of Fairtrade Cocoa

Mayan farmers in Toledo, Belize have always grown cocoa for personal use. In the 1980s, USAid (US Agency for International Development) proposed that these farmers abandon the native breed they have been growing organically for thousands of years, replacing it with a hybrid seed requiring chemical fertilisers and pesticides. These would have to be bought using cash they would have to raise by mortgaging their land.

Whilst demand for cocoa was rising, the price was falling due to increased global supply. In 1993, when the trees were at last bearing fruit, US company Hershey offered the farmers just 33.5 cents per pound, significantly less than the 85 cents per pound in the US Aid proposal five years previously.

Craig Sams, co-founder of Green & Black's chocolate, who had recently visited a cocoa plantation in Belize was, at that point, branching out from his job running Whole Earth foods to found Green & Black's. He had noted that many of the farmers had spurned (or been unable to afford) USAid's seeds, fertilisers and pesticides, and had mostly stuck to traditional organic farming of the indigenous cocoa.

When Sams discovered that the Toledo farmers had lost their American buyer, he offered to buy their beans for 63 cents a pound - roughly 10% higher than the market rate at the time. He promised to continue buying at this price, year on year, regardless of downward variations in the market. Should the market price rise, he would adjust his price upwards to match it. This promise, originally made to Toledan cocoa farmers in November 1993, was to become the bedrock of the Fairtrade philosophy.

Green & Black's was bought by Cadbury Schweppes in 2005. At the time of writing in 2008, just one of its 13 varieties of chocolate carries the Fairtrade certification.

of various shaped boxes filled with Italian delights from the delicatessen. Tom was literally salivating with delight as he peered into the boxes.

"Why don't you go and watch a little telly and I'll get all this prepared – it shouldn't take long."

Tom didn't need asking twice, and as Laura busied herself in their small kitchen, he found some football on the TV and settled himself down on the sofa.

Before long, Laura had laid the table, complete with candles, and displayed the antipasti, along with some Italian oils and a small loaf of focaccia bread. The pasta was still bubbling on the stove when she called Tom to join her at the table.

"Oh, babe, this looks great – today must have gone really well, eh?"

Laura knew that she couldn't put off telling Tom any longer. She passed him the antipasti plate.

"Well, it didn't quite go according to plan."

"What do you mean?"

"Well, I made a bit of an error in judgement. But I didn't realise it until it was too late."

"Riiigghht" said Tom slowly – he could sense bad news coming. "So what happened?"

"Well, I basically suggested to JJ that we launch the ethical bar, but that to make it more cost-effective, we didn't just use fairly traded chocolate – we used regular chocolate too."

"You what? Are you mad? The fact that it's fairly traded is the whole point – that's the reason that people buy it!"

Changing Institutional Mistrust

In January 2001, Paul Wilson took on the mantle of Chief Executive at St Philips Chambers in Birmingham. Over the next five years, the Chambers grew from a turnover of £8 million to £18.5 million. Coming from the banking world, Paul was surprised by the barristers' clerks' traditional practices. Many clerks had started their training at just 16 years of age and had developed a conscience that was content with what would be regarded in 'normal' commerce as untruths. In an environment in which a large number of court cases collapse, the clerks would habitually double-book barristers' court appearances, knowing that they may well have to let a solicitor client down at the last minute if the original case did proceed.

Keen to establish real customer trust, Paul did away with this practice, imposing clear standards of behaviour, and enforcing those standards across the practice. The clerks learnt to be more open with clients by explaining their barrister's limited availability and working openly with the solicitors to find a solution. Whilst in the short-term, this meant some levels of confusion and apparent loss of lucrative work, in due course it generated valuable repeat business as solicitors understood that the clerks were being straightforward. Over time, a culture of 'agreed / institutional' mistrust was replaced with a culture of trust. St Philips is now thought to be the biggest Chambers in the world by barrister number.

"Yes, thanks Tom, I know that" replied Laura, slightly riled.

"Honestly, Laura, that's career suicide. You suggested that you lie to your customers!" Tom laughed. Laura didn't appreciate his jesting.

"So what did JJ say? Did he ask you to go back to the drawing board?"

"No. JJ didn't say much. He shouted a lot though. And he went very red" Laura said, collecting herself before she could say the words out loud.

"Then he fired me."

"He what?"

"He fired me. He said that what I was suggesting was deceiving our customers, and that wasn't the 'Gabriels way'. Then he fired me. He fired me, Tom." Laura dropped the fork that she had been toying with and it fell to the china plate with a crash.

"I haven't got a job. I haven't got a car. I've barely got a reputation. How could I have been so stupid?"

Tom got up from his seat and knelt beside his girlfriend and hugged her. She buried her head in his chest and sobbed. She bawled her eyes out.

She'd been leading up to this all day.

Tom affectionately stroked her hair in an attempt to console her. He had seen this day coming; the Laura whom he had fallen in love with at university had changed. She had become too focused on her goals, consumed by her

Explosive change of heart

In 1867, a Swedish chemist discovered dynamite. Before long, his creation was patented in every developed country. By 1880, he was head of the largest dynamite producing cartel in the world. He amassed enormous wealth from royalties and dividends, then, one day, in 1888 a French newspaper confused the death of his brother with his own. The tycoon had the rare opportunity to read his own obituary. Phrases like 'the merchant of death is dead' and 'fortune amassed by finding new ways to mutilate and kill' challenged him to question his apparent success.

From that moment on, Alfred Nobel vowed to live the rest of his life another way, by establishing a prize for those who achieved success not through wealth, but through science, the arts and peace. He died in 1896 leaving a legacy equivalent to $104,000,000 in today's money to fund the Nobel Prizes.

career, become blinded by the trappings of success that comes with it, and in the process had lost sight of what was important. She had lost sight of the ethics, the morals, the values, that her parents had brought her up to respect. He had hoped that in time she would have seen this for herself, rather than have all her dreams crash down around her so spectacularly.

66 *'Relationships' is not just another business buzzword. Learning to do business relationally is bringing great benefits both to our organisation and to our clients.* **99**

Paul O'Donnell, Ogilvy One

Thursday evening came and, as agreed, Laura met Steve at his delicatessen.

"So, where are we going?"

"Oh, somewhere quite special. Well, it's somewhere quite simple, but very special."

"Sounds intriguing!"

"Well, I think you'll find it interesting – come on, let's go. It's not far."

Steve led Laura around the corner to his little van, painted the same blue as the delicatessen.

"My days of the shiny company car are gone, as you can see" said Steve, with just a hint of disappointment in his voice.

"Don't worry, so are mine!" said Laura, laughing.

"Hop in!"

Before long, the pair had reached the outskirts of town, and Steve pulled up outside a very unassuming restaurant which stood alone, just off the main road. What was Steve talking about? Laura thought to herself. This didn't look very special at all. She glanced above the door – Otis' Eats was written in fluorescent tubing above the windows of the restaurant. It really didn't look much from the outside.

Steve could see that Laura was none too impressed, and let his amusement show on his face.

Snapshots

"If we're going to have a banking relationship,
you'll have to trust me more than this."

"What!" exclaimed Laura mockingly, noticing Steve's wry smile.

"You corporate girls! I don't know, take you away from your expense account restaurants with the starched linen napkins and fawning Maître D's and you're lost! This is real life, Laura. And besides, you shouldn't judge a book by its cover - wait until you get inside. It's something quite special. And I don't just mean the food."

The outside and the inside of the restaurant couldn't have been more different. The place was packed. Tables of different sizes were scattered everywhere – and every single one occupied. And not occupied with your typical early evening diner, either. This place attracted quite a cross section of different clientele - families, couples, business people, teenagers celebrating birthdays, older people. Everyone was chatting and laughing, and there were a few children running between tables, yet no-one seemed to mind. The place had a distinct feel to it. Relaxed, friendly, comfortable. And there was a tangible authenticity to it – there was no contrived image or atmosphere. Each table was covered in a bright, garish tablecloth with a jug, not a vase, of flowers. The chairs were all different, as was the crockery - nothing seemed to match. And rather than the usual piped music, there was a lady sitting on a stool in the corner of the restaurant playing her guitar and singing songs. There were no corporate uniforms here - in fact, expressing individuality seemed to be the order of the day. A waiter with pink spiky hair, carrying a dish of casserole squeezed past Laura. "S'cuse me!"

Emotional purchases

Decisions are made in the blink of an eye and consumers are persuaded by their emotions without even realising it. Understanding the role of emotions in human decision making and behaviour will help marketers to gain better understanding of the needs and barriers of consumers.

It is in the cingulated cortex region of the brain that decisions are made: reason and emotion accumulate, allowing us to coordinate our emotional response to direct our thoughts and actions. Critically, the decision-making process cannot work in the absence of an emotional signal from the limbic system. The implications of this for marketers are inescapable.

But here, somehow, it just all seemed to work. It was unusual, but it had oodles of charm.

"Well, this is different!" said Laura smiling, teasing Steve with a slightly sarcastic tone in her voice.

He chose to ignore it. "It is, isn't it. My wife and I found this place about a year or so ago, and we've got very friendly with the owner; in fact, he helped me to get my head around leaving the protection of corporate life at Gabriels to open up the deli."

"That would be Otis, then?" said Laura, nudging her head in the direction of the large neon sign on the wall opposite them – a constant pink, dusty, neon reminder to everyone where they were, lest they forgot.

"Indeed. Otis is a great guy. Amazing. He's built a profitable business that is genuinely loved by his customers. But the thing that I most admire about him, Laura, is that he has done so without compromising on his personal values. In fact, if anything, he's capitalised on them and made them central to his business."

Laura looked away with an embarrassed look on her face. Steve's effusive description of Otis emphasised the predicament Laura was in, and reminded her of the mistake that she had made in disregarding her own values.

"No, no, Laura, I wasn't trying to make a point or embarrass you" said Steve quickly, seeing the playfulness suddenly disappear from Laura's face.

"It's fine, Steve, really, it's fine."

"It's just that Otis' values are absolutely central to his business. Absolutely central."

Trust Pays

In a study carried out by A&R Business Group Inc. (www.bccq.org), 6,500 employees from Holiday Inn International Hotels were surveyed to determine architects of trust, and the results were correlated with personnel records, customer satisfaction scores and hotel revenues. Hotels where managers were perceived to follow through on their promises were found to be more profitable, and it was estimated that a 12.5% improvement in employee trust ratings should improve hotel profitability by $250,000 annually.

"How can they be? What do you mean?" Laura was intrigued. How could a man's values be so evident when he ran a restaurant? Short of making a big deal about serving locally grown vegetables and organic meat? Laura wanted to know more.

"Well, he…"

"Steve!"

Steve was just about to answer when he was accosted by a man who had bounded toward him, seemingly from nowhere. The two men gave each other a warm bear hug, slapping each other affectionately on the back. Emerging from the hug, the man gave Steve a kiss on the cheek, much to Laura's surprise. She watched the pair with interest. She wasn't quite expecting what she saw before her. Late thirties, the man was dressed like a Californian surfer. Flip flops, baggy ripped jeans, a tight T-shirt, with long, blonde dreadlocks tied in a huge knot behind his head - Laura didn't come into contact with people like this very often. And neither, she had thought, did Steve. Clearly, she was wrong. "Hey, Steve, great to see you - how are you doing?"

"I'm great, great. It's good to see you, man!" said Steve, warmly.

Since when did Steve call people 'man' thought Laura to herself.

"Otis - I've brought someone along for you to meet. This is Laura - she's been in the wars recently at work and I wanted to bring her here so that she can experience your own special way of doing business firsthand. She needs to

Trusted sources of information

The Edelman Annual Trust Barometer is the largest study of credibility and trust known to date. Now in its eighth year, the 2007 study surveyed 3,100 opinion leaders from across 18 countries, and identified the latest trends in trust across institutions, companies and sources of information.

Key finding - Source credibility

In 11 of the 18 countries, business magazines are the most, or second most, trusted sources of information about a company. 'Conversations with friends and peers' is as trusted a source of information about a company as 'articles in newspapers' or 'television news coverage'. Traditional media sources such as newspapers, TV, and radio remain more credible than new media sources such as a company website or an internet blog.

be converted to your unique approach!"
"Ah yes, I remember when I first met you, Steve – it was like a revelation to you, wasn't it? Hallelujah, brother!"
Steve laughed and pushed his friend playfully.
"Yeah, yeah, all right!'
Laura extended her hand. "Hi. Good to meet you."
Otis laughed. "We don't do handshakes here, lover," and before Laura could really take in what was happening, she found herself engulfed in a hug, squashing her outstretched hand.
She could hear Steve chuckling behind her.
"Come on Otis, have you got a table for us?" asked Steve, patting his friend on the back as he squeezed Laura.
"Sure – now that you've been officially welcomed, Laura" winked Otis.
He bounded into the centre of the restaurant, the two following him. Otis found them a table that had just been vacated by a couple of lovestruck teenagers on a date, and cleared away the last of the glasses and bowls while Laura and Steve sat down.
"Ok, specials are on the board, straight menus are right here. You'll get your food in around twenty minutes, but don't hold me to that, and I'll bring you over a jug of water in a second. The pork and apple casserole is really good today, and we've got special cheddar mash and fresh peas from Jimmy's farm just down the road with that. But there are lots of other options on the menu if you don't fancy that. Back in a mo'." And with that, he was gone.
Laura sighed with gusto. "I'm exhausted!"

Corporate Social Responsibility Is Not New

The twenty first century has had more than its fair share of corporate scandals, followed by a tide of new policies and practices to attempt to clean up the image of commerce. Not for the first time, following the industrial revolution at the start of the last century, a number of entrepreneurs with a conscience built businesses such as Cadbury and Rowntree with a social conscience. In her book Body and Soul, the late founder of The Body Shop, Anita Roddick wrote *"I am still looking for the modern day equivalent of those Quakers who ran successful businesses, made money because they offered honest products and treated their people decently, worked hard themselves, spent honestly, saved honestly, gave honest value for their money, put back more than they took out and told no lies."*

"Yes, quite a character, isn't he?"

"Goodness, I'll say!" replied Laura laughing. "Sweet, though, and I can see what you mean about values – what you see is definitely what you get!"

Steve smiled. "Yes, but that's not it!"

"What do you mean? What else is there?"

"Oh, that would spoil the fun! I'll let you work that one out for yourself" teased Steve, as he adopted a faux mysterious look and slowly buried his head in the menu, smiling as his eyes disappeared from her view.

"What are you like?" laughed Laura, scanning the menu. She had forgotten how much fun Steve was. The pork sounded very good, but she was often tempted by specials, and then regretted it afterwards when she saw how good other people's food looked when it arrived at the table. She wanted to make sure that there were no more tempting options to be had.

"Hang on" said Laura, lifting her head from the menu and looking around the restaurant, sweeping her head from side to side like an animal who has heard something unusual in the undergrowth. "There are no prices on the menu. There are no prices on the specials' board." She checked the menu again. "There are no prices!"

Steve laughed out loud. "Hallelujah!"

Laura looked confused. "Hey? How can there be no prices?"

"You're right – there are no prices. And that's an integral part of what Otis does here. Oh, talk of the devil." At that moment, Otis arrived back at the table with a large jug

66 The growing trust in 'people like me' and average employers means that companies must design their communications as much on the horizontal or the peer to peer axis as on the vertical top-down axis. CEOs should continue to talk with elites such as investors and regulators, but also provide critical information to employees and enthusiastic consumers who spur the peer-to-peer discussion. Third parties with credentials, like academics and physicians are also critical. 99

David Brain, President and CEO of Edelman Europe

of water brimming with lemon and ice. It hit the table with a thud and, as he looked up from getting out his pad and paper, he found his two diners looking at him expectantly.

He furrowed his brow suspiciously. "What?"

"Laura has just discovered your unique differentiator" said Steve, inviting Otis to take the floor. Smiling, Otis didn't need asking twice. He pulled up a chair and joined the pair at the small table, immediately increasing its cosiness quotient.

"Ok, ask away, fair maiden."

"Steve told me before I came here that ethics and values were integral to your business, and when I came here and I saw the people that work here, the quirkiness of the place, and, dare I say, met you, I thought that that was where the values were at play. You know – being laid back, slightly kooky, super-friendly, serving really good home cooked food – I thought that was it. I would have thought that was it, to be honest – that's all so unusual on its own. So, why no prices?"

Otis gave Steve a smile. "It had this one foxed the first time he came here too!" he said affectionately, nodding his head towards his friend.

Steve blushed a little and looked at the table.

"For me, it's quite simple" Otis began. "From time to time I would go to a restaurant for a meal and then get the bill and just think 'that wasn't worth it'. Perhaps the food quality wasn't up to scratch, or there wasn't enough of it, but I would be presented with the bill and I would have

Radiohead adopt pay what it's worth approach

UK rock band Radiohead released their seventh studio album *In Rainbows* online in October 2007, ahead of a physical CD release in shops. The band took the unusual step of asking those who downloaded the music to pay whatever they felt the album was worth between £0 and £100. During the first 29 days of October, 1.2 million people visited the *In Rainbows* website. Although several reportedly paid nothing, the average price paid was £2.90. Critics have argued that the experiment was therefore a failure, although it should be noted that when the CD was later released in January 2008, it went straight to number one in the CD sales charts. Other benefits to the band include a broadening fan base, significant goodwill and a wealth of listener feedback.

to pay it, no matter what I actually thought of the food. Of course, if there is something wrong with the food, like the fish is off, for example, then you complain and make the appropriate noises and it gets taken off your bill. But I'm not talking about that – I'm talking about those times when you sit there and look at the bill and just think 'that just wasn't good value for money', for whatever reason."

Laura was transfixed. There was something very compelling about Otis; his passion was very attractive.

"So, I got to thinking one day that there was a certain amount of arrogance associated with pricing in restaurants. And, come to think of it, almost anything you pay for. So I spent some significant time thinking about this. Laura, let me ask you a question." Laura nodded her agreement.

"Who's going to be eating your meal?" Laura looked at Steve, and then back at Otis, unsure of what to answer. It seemed such a painfully obvious question. Was she missing something?

"Well, I am" she said hesitantly, her eyes flitting between the two men, looking for validation.

"Right. You are the one who is enjoying the food. You are the one savouring the flavours. You are the one having the experience. So who am I, as the restauranteur – the person not eating the meal – to tell you how much you're enjoying it?" Otis paused for a second to allow Laura a moment to reflect on his idea.

"But restaurant pricing isn't about how much you enjoy the food, it's about how much it costs. Isn't it?"

"Is it? So how come that cheeseburger at the drive thru

Trust elicits trust - and the reverse is also true, distrust fosters distrust.

1. X's decision to trust enhances X's trust – this happens due to cognitive dissonance reduction.
2. X's trusting decision enhances Y's trustworthiness – X's decision to trust may enhance Y's self-confidence and goodwill because he feels more responsibilities upon himself.
3. If X trusts Y, Y will probably end up trusting X – when X makes himself dependent on Y, X becomes trustworthy for Y because X is facing risks. X appears trustworthy leading to Y's decision to trust X also.
4. If X trusts Y, other agents will probably also trust Y – the fact that X trusts Y could induce others to trust Y, also starting a process of spreading trust towards Y.

Reference - research from T3 Group, a research team hosted in the Institute of Cognitive Sciences and Technologies (ISTC) http://www.istc.cnr.it/T3/trust/pages/dynamics.html

when you have a cheeseburger craving is so cheap? Sitting in the car and sinking your teeth into that steaming, freshly cooked burger with freshly melted Swiss cheese may be the most satisfying meal you've had in ages. But it cost you peanuts."

Laura nodded gently. She couldn't fault Otis' logic.

"Then you go to the fancy-schmancy restaurant, and you eat a small, but perfectly formed and perfectly choreographed meal, yet you walk out of there having blown a small fortune and feel nowhere near as satisfied as you do eating that cheeseburger. That didn't make sense to me."

"So what you're saying is that it's about perceived value?"

"Well, yes, partly. I mean, I just thought that it was arrogant to charge someone a certain amount for a meal, completely disregarding their enjoyment of that meal. And because I think that there is a very strong correlation between the quality of that meal, and someone's enjoyment of that meal. Which is why we stick to tried and tested recipes, serve family favourite dishes and generous portions, and make sure that we source our ingredients as locally as we can to ensure quality."

"There is a logic to that – I can't deny it. Surely this isn't all free – I know you couldn't run a business like that. So how do people know what to pay?"

Steve, who was sitting quietly and enjoying watching Laura's baptism, butted in "Now here's the clever bit!"

Otis paused, then looked Laura straight in the eye.

"I ask the customers to leave what they feel the meal is worth."

The real pay-what-you-like restaurant

For over 15 years, a small French style restaurant in north London has been full most nights, despite never displaying a price on its menu. When Vasos Michael, a Cypriot immigrant, decided to set up a restaurant in this residential suburb, he had faith that the local community wouldn't take advantage of his trusting approach to pricing.

Years later he's been proved right as his takings exceed those of comparable restaurants, and his reputation is known far and wide. Tourists regularly make the 40 minute trip from the centre of the city to visit the eatery, with one group of four Americans paying £600 for their meal.

Otis sat back in his chair, stretched out his legs, and put his hands behind his head, waiting for Laura's response - which he was sure would follow the pattern he had experienced after explaining this same story countless times previously to curious business people.

"You do what?" exclaimed Laura, almost choking on her words.

Otis smiled and repeated himself. "I ask the customers to leave what they think the meal is worth." He and Steve exchanged a knowing smile across the small table.

"You can't run a business like that!"

"Oh, really? Who says?" challenged Otis.

"Well, you just can't."

"Yeah – great argument!" he laughed.

"Well, you can't! How do you make any money?"

"Oh don't worry about that, Laura, I make plenty of money. In fact, the place is never empty from eight o'clock in the morning until 10 o'clock at night. My takings are up 30% on last year."

Laura looked at the two men incredulously. "I don't see how that can be?"

"Well, let me explain. To put it simply, I provide a great environment, a consistent delicious product, and friendly service. People like coming here – they come back time after time – they like the staff, they like the food, they feel comfortable here, and they pay accordingly. Now, I'm not a complete fool…" - Laura raised an eyebrow at this comment - "…because I know that people have a general view of how much a meal like the one they enjoy here

"Look...people are basically honest and decent. Why don't we scrap the tax laws completely and have the people pay whatever they think is fair?"

would cost them elsewhere – so they do have a benchmark. But they then use that benchmark to leave an amount of money that they feel their meal here, and experience, is worth."

"Ok, well, what if they leave nothing?" challenged Laura

"You know, that has never happened."

"But people must leave ridiculously small amounts."

"On occasion, that does happen, but we make sure that we recognise them, and if they come back, which they rarely do, then I'll have a casual chat with them before they order, just so that they understand how the land lies – I ask them to respect us and our business as much as we are respecting them by giving them an 'open charge' policy, as I like to call it."

"And that works?"

"That works."

"But you could make so much more money if you charged proper prices on the menus."

Otis laughed. "Well, that assumes that I'm running this restaurant to simply make money."

"Well, aren't you? Why else would you be in business?"

"I'm in business because I want to provide for people. And because this is the kind of restaurant that I wanted to eat in – and there was nothing like it available. The open charge policy has become part of our charm, and people understand that we are baring our chest to them. It's that honesty, that vulnerability, that trust, that people respond to."

Laura was speechless. She understood everything that Otis

High Trust Organisations experience:

- half the average staff turnover of industry peers
- higher productivity and profitability
- more qualified candidates for open positions
- higher levels of customer satisfaction and loyalty
- more adaptive organisational structures
- constructive strategic alliances
- responsive virtual teams
- effective crisis management
- reduced transaction and litigation costs

(As reported by A&R Brown Business Group Inc.)

was saying, yet it was a mismatch with what she had been taught in business school. There it was all about profit, turnover, and pushing and pushing your agenda until either the customers bought it, or the product died. But here the approach to business was quite different, and was clearly successful - 30% increase in turnover in a year was not to be sniffed at. Laura would have killed for results like that when she was at Gabriels.

The man with the pink spiky hair arrived at the table, armed with plates of steaming food.

"Danny – right on cue!" Otis moved aside for the food to be laid on the table. It looked good. Both Laura and Steve had picked up their knife and fork almost before the plates had hit the table.

"Tuck in! said Otis, before he turned and disappeared into the crowded restaurant.

❝ *Trust is crucial to the success of ecomomic relationships such as that between managers and workers, or between companies and their suppliers, and honesty is the essential lubricant to a system of exchange.* **❞**

Richard Bronk, in *The Invisible Hand*

Otis' Eats had thinned out considerably since they sat down at their table, quite some time ago now. The staff were cleaning tables around the last few diners who were lingering over their coffees, and the restaurant was visibly emptying out. Laura loved to 'people watch', but her observations today were fuelled by a different interest – she was intrigued with what Otis had told her earlier, and she had watched when people settled up for their meals – how much did they leave? Laura did a quick calculation every time that she saw someone leaving money, and Otis was right. People did leave roughly what she would have expected to pay in other restaurants – and, often times, more. This was quite a new experience for her. This place was achieving something quite special.

"So, how was it?" Otis asked. Having left his staff to look after the last few customers, he had pulled up a chair to join his two friends.

"It was great. Really good, thank you," said Laura. "And very interesting too – I was watching people when they left, and you're right – they do leave very sensible, even generous, amounts."

"Yes – once people discover us, they quickly become regulars. Some would say we are very fortunate, but I believe that we reap what we sow. We gave people an

Guidelines for trust

1. Trust is a two-way street; you get it if you give it

2. Sometimes people don't trust you because of the actions of a person close to you

3. Sometimes trust has to be earned

4. In order to fix broken trust, both sides have to want the trust back

5. Trust is an essential part of ALL successful relationships

6. Trust is a gift – you give it and receive it, but you should never take it for granted

alternative to the assumptive arrogance of other restaurants – we trust them, and they rarely betray that trust. In fact, I've found that it brings out the best in people."

"Didn't you do a study a while ago?" prompted Steve.

"Oh yes, thanks, that's right" said Otis, nodding appreciatively to his friend. "I annotated a menu with prices that I would expect people to pay in regular restaurants, and then, for a month, at the end of each day I would go through what each table had consumed and what they had felt compelled to pay for it. I would then compare that to the prices on the menu. And you know what? On average, people left 18% more than they would have been asked to do by the menu. So, trusting people and giving them the freedom to leave what they thought the meal was worth, gave me 18% more revenue than I would have got if I ran a standard restaurant with a standard menu, where I dictated to people what the meal that they enjoyed was worth. Laura, you looked gobsmacked earlier when I explained what I do here – amazed as to how I could sustain a business by using this approach. Well, this place is testament to the fact that by trusting people to place their own worth on the experience that I provide for them, they repay that trust with even greater rewards. Trust is essential. It is quite simply the heart of my business."

Laura sat thoughtfully, toying with her teaspoon. "I see that" she sighed, looking at Steve. "I think my approach to business needs a little open heart surgery."

66 *Man's goodness is a flame that can be hidden but never extinguished* **99**

Nelson Mandela

After kissing Tom on his way to work the next morning, Laura lay in bed and stared out of the window, watching the clouds drift by, and listening to the faint sound of birdsong from the nearby tree. As her thoughts turned to work, Laura glanced at the bedside clock. 8am. Usually, she would be well on her way to work by now, sitting comfortably in her BMW with the rest of the morning rushhour traffic, on the way to her office at Gabriels. While the rest of the world was going about their daily business, she sighed deeply and pulled the warm duvet up around her chin.

How had it come to this?

She lay in silence and reflected on the few short years since she had started work. Where had young Laura gone? Where was the little girl who would cry every time her father killed a fly? Who baked cakes and sold them at her stall on the driveway so she could give the money to the children's home? Where was the young woman who campaigned for government aid for third world poverty at university? Who cared about something other than herself?

Laura felt a tear gently touch her cheek as she watched herself in her mind's eye. Redirecting that huge delivery of Dairy Gold, as good as blackmailing her way into getting a BMW, buying her expensive handbag and damaging her

Mutually Acceptable

As trust in corporate institutions diminishes, a renewed engagement with mutuals is anticipated. Whereas a typical bank or insurance company is owned by shareholders, mutuals exist solely for the benefit of their members. These members are both the customers and the owners. Rather than generating dividends for anonymous shareholders, good financial performance is reflected in lower premiums in the case of insurance or better interest rates in the case of savings and loan organisations, commonly known as Building Societies in the UK.

One limitation on the mutual is the inability to sell equity to raise money for expansion or to fund a lean period. The 2008 credit crunch put the mutual philosophy to the test.

relationship with Tom. Suggesting that JJ betray his loyal customers by selling an ethical chocolate bar that wasn't 'quite' ethical.

Laura felt her stomach churn as she relived her catastrophic experience in the Boardroom.

Where had it all gone wrong? What had she become?

She knew that she had to do something.

She turned her thoughts to Steve. A chance meeting, she had seen how content he was with his new life running the delicatessen. And the approach that he was taking with the way he sourced his products, served his customers, ran his business. Steve's words echoed in Laura's head. Business isn't about products and services and stuff a lot of the time. It's all about feelings, emotions and relationships.

Otis drifted into Laura's thoughts. Eccentric and independent, she recalled the packed restaurant and the wonderful food served by the guy with pink, spiky hair. She smiled as she remembered. The straightforward authenticity was refreshing. Otis' parting words to her were ringing in her ears: "Trust is essential. It is, quite simply, the heart of my business."

"That's it" she said to herself.

Laura slowly sat up in bed, almost hypnotised by her own thoughts. "It's all about the trust. It's the backbone of a business – it's got to be. Every product picked off the shelf, every meal ordered in a restaurant, is an exercise in trust. It's everywhere – it's the invisible thread that holds everything together. Everything. It's everywhere." It was

Self-interest, the antithesis of trust

To assess the trustworthiness of a person or organisation, this fast and accurate assessment should be used. We don't rely on trustworthy behaviour alone, but instead explore the true motives or the level of self-interest within the other party, best described by the formula below:

$$\text{Trustworthiness} = \frac{\text{Relationship, Credibility, Dependability}}{\text{Self-Interest}}$$

Adapted from Maister, Green & Galfords' trust equation found in
The Trusted Advisor, Free Press 2001

All too often a person or brand will exhibit behaviours that give confidence, only to disappoint at a later date when their true intentions come under threat.

all finally making sense to her.

"JJ was right. It was the essential ingredient. Without trust, there can be no business. Without trust, there's nothing."

With that, and with an expression on her face as if she had won the lottery, Laura jumped out of her bed and ran towards the bathroom.

"Of course it was almost ethical. There was one essential missing ingredient. Trust!"

❝ *Trust may sometimes need to operate without the feeling of confidence.* **❞**

C. S. Lewis

The sound of the tannoy dominated the terminal.

"Will the last remaining passengers for Virgin Atlantic flight 651 to Lagos, Nigeria, please proceed to Gate 67."

Laura collected up her papers and magazines from the counter, stuffed them into her hand luggage, and made her way towards the gate.

She had had a revelation lying in bed that morning a few short days ago. Laura had pinpointed where she had gone wrong. She had mixed her recipe for success without one vital ingredient: trust. She had forgotten the importance of trust in her relationship with her employers, her boss, her customers, and even her boyfriend. Contemplating her future in bed that morning, she had decided that she was going to repair her integrity. She was going to find a way of rising to the challenge that JJ had originally set her and by doing so, rehabilitate herself, her approach to her work, and perhaps, if she was totally honest, even her approach to herself. She wasn't proud of the person that she had become. Perhaps this was the route to her salvation.

After somehow managing to persuade Tom to let her use a significant portion of their wedding savings to fund her trip to the Ivory Coast, Laura was on her way. She knew she was lucky to have such an understanding fiancé, and one

The Virgin Factor

Virgin's greatest asset is arguably not a $200 million aircraft, it is Richard Branson and the 'Virgin people' that make up the organisation. Branson's charismatic style and entrepreneurial flair is an asset that other organisations can't replicate; it is his personality that is synonymous with the Virgin brand, and that makes the company unique. Similarly, the Virgin Group attracts 'Virgin people', who are 'only a certain type.' Together with Branson, the 'Virgin people' form the human capital that is distinctive to Virgin, and impossible for other companies to copy.

Related to the people who make up the firm is the 'Virgin culture' that has been built over decades, and that distinguishes the work environment within the Virgin Group from other organisations. It is a culture that is 'not looking for clones,' that is 'like a family', and is one that requires employees to have the 'Virgin flair.' These unique attributes present in Virgin employees weld together to create a distinctive corporate culture that only the Virgin Group can claim to have.

"I come up with the original idea, spend the first three months immersed in the business so I know the ins and outs, and then give chief executives a stake in the company and ask them to run it as if it's their own," explains Branson. "I intervene as little as possible. Give them that, and they will give everything back."

Richard Branson's personality is synonymous with Virgin's strong branding and reputation. The brand was 'recognised by 96 percent of UK consumers' and is associated amongst consumers with 'fun, innovation, success and trust.'

who trusted her when she said that this "was something she just had to do." She had no job, no sniff of a job in the near future, and yet she wanted to go to Africa to try and achieve the goal that had led to her downfall from Gabriels: to create a mass market, competitively priced, truly ethical chocolate bar. She was truly blessed. The amount of trust and belief that Tom was demonstrating in her by letting her do this was overwhelming. The contrast with her own recent behaviour wasn't lost on her. Instead of taking Tom for granted as she had done for so long, she did, in fact, have much to learn from him.

66 *Trust is a resource that increases through use.* **99**

Anon

"Did you want the chicken or fish?"

Laura was gently woken from a catnap by the Virgin stewardess. She opened her eyes to a warm smile and, as she righted herself in her seat, crumpled the map which was covering her chest and lap. She had fallen asleep whilst she reviewed her route planning from Lagos to where she knew she would find what she was looking for.

Realising that she was holding up the rest of her row, Laura shook herself into action. "Sorry, looks like I fell straight asleep!"

Laura grabbed the menu card that she had placed down the side of her seat earlier, and quickly scanned the options. She read the two descriptions of the main course, and as she noticed that the fish was 'from the Lochaire fishery in the highlands of Scotland, specially selected for their revolutionary approach to organically farmed fish', she smiled and giggled under her breath.

As this wasn't the reaction that the stewardess usually received when she asked a customer to make their menu selection, she was a little bemused, but disguised it well with her professional smile. "Is everything alright?" she enquired hesitantly, conscious that Laura's dithering had begun to attract the attention of her hungry fellow travellers in the immediate vicinity.

Unnecessary Procedures

Most organisations contain unnecessary procedures and processes. Until relatively recently, if you were travelling by air you weren't allowed to check in without a ticket. Then someone new to the industry pointed out that the bookings are all stored on the computer system and the ticket was really just a form of identification. Why not use a more reliable form of identification like a passport, which very often passengers carry with them, and do away with printed tickets and the associated expense that they generate.

"Oh yes, everything is just fine. I think I'd better take the fish, thank you." And with that, Laura was passed her tray with her fish steaming in front of her, along with a rather compact-looking salad in a plastic box, a provocatively delicious-looking chocolate dessert, and various accoutrements in a plastic sleeve.

The flight from London was a long one and, as she had booked the Lagos flight just days beforehand, Laura had not had much time to plan the onward journey that she would need to make after she touched down in Lagos. She had been here once before. At least once a year, a small group of Buyers from Gabriels would take a buying trip to the Ivory Coast and meet up with the cocoa buyers - meeting growers, tasting beans, and negotiating their supplies of the best quality raw materials that their budgets would allow for the next nine to 12 months. This would allow the Buyers to forecast their production and profit margins, whilst also allowing the Brand Managers, like Laura, to gain a full understanding of the industry. The whole process was symbiotic, and in many ways, like a house of cards – price increases from the beginning of the chain would have a ripple effect right through the chain, from the grower to the Buyer to the Brand Manager to the retailer, and finally through to the customer, who would inevitably feel it the most. And this was something that the Gabriels team worked hard to avoid. They wanted to give their customers the best quality products for the keenest price – which was why these trips were so crucial. Brand

Negotiation

Every sales manual ever printed talks about 'rapport'; it's a vital ingredient to reaching agreement. As anyone who has ever tried to sell by telephone will tell you, it's a much harder task to establish rapport when you can't see the eyes of the person you are dealing with.

Face-to-face contact conveys enthusiasm, concern, knowledge, and confidence much more quickly than can ever be achieved by a telephone conversation or series of emails. So having got up close and personal with your supplier or customer how do you reach the right outcome?

- Set out to build a relationship and solve a problem
- Know your goals
- Do your homework
- Be always curious, never furious
- Hear not just the words but also the actions (body language)

Managers rarely had the opportunity to travel on trips like this, but Laura, back in her heyday at Gabriels when she was one of JJ's protégées, was given the opportunity by JJ himself, who wanted to give her a rounded view of the business and ensure that she appreciated the importance and impact of this chain. How times had changed! Laura doubted that JJ would even take her call now if she contacted him.

Still, from that sole trip she made, she had learned a great deal about the growers and the process of buying, and was now determined to find a grower who would be able to partner with her and supply the beans that would enable her to realise her dream of creating an authentically fairly traded chocolate bar at the best possible quality, and for a price that would make it a real alternative to all the standard chocolate bars on the market. She wanted to put right the mistake that she had made in the Boardroom. Secretly, she held out hope that if she was somehow able to pull this off, JJ may take her back. She knew that this was a long shot, and she daren't even think about it consciously for fear that somehow she might jinx even the possibility.

Retrieving the crumpled map that she had quickly pushed into the footwell while she ate her supper, Laura followed the route that she had begun to mark on the map with an orange fluorescent pen. It was to be quite a journey, and would take her a good few days after landing at Lagos. She was prepared though – she had booked a Toyota Land Cruiser from a contact in Lagos, and that would be waiting

Why is Toyota on Top?

Toyota is consistently ranked as the most respected and admired motor company around the world, known for their cars' impeccable reliability, derived from an uncompromising approach to manufacturing. Toyota don't keep this to themselves though; they operate a code of openness with their supply chain where they share best practice and, in turn, expect equivalent levels of transparency from those who sell to them.

It's not at all unusual for a new supplier to have his manufacturing processes examined and improved at Toyota's expense. One supplier commented: *"Naturally we feel indebted to Toyota and view them as a special customer; they sincerely want to help us improve."*

Like other Japanese businesses, Toyota will often invest in a minority stake in their suppliers' companies, not to gain control, but instead to prove their long-term commitment and shared aspirations. It's thought that Toyota's procurement costs in the United States are 20% that of General Motors' expenditure.

It's this uncompromising approach to product quality and long-term business performance that has made Toyota the most profitable motor manufacturer on the planet.

for her when she landed early in the morning. Some of the journey would be on makeshift roads, which could be treacherous in places, and Laura knew that she would need transport which was durable if she was to arrive at her destination in good time, and in one piece.

66 *Where there is trust there is hope.* **99**

Charles Handy, writer

After landing at Murtala Muhammed airport at 6am and wrestling with the crowds at the airport - where it appeared customary for every family member for generations to be at the airport to welcome their traveller home - Laura was reunited with her luggage, a fairly compact rucksack, and made her way towards her rented Land Cruiser. Laura felt like she had entered another world – even though she was still in the airport compound; she could see, feel, and hear the difference with the world that she had left behind her just 12 hours ago. The heat was stifling, and she had forgotten how overpowering the hustle and bustle of this busy African airport could be. Stopping to take a look at the majestic scenery as she loaded her bags into the 4x4, she smiled. It felt good to be back, and at that moment she was filled with an overwhelming sense of optimism.

Laura's journey took her through the jungle terrain to Ghana and then, after a short break, onto the Bas Sassandra region of the Ivory Coast. Laura had learnt from her colleagues during her one previous trip that this was the place to find not only the best quality cocoa beans, but also the greatest choice of growers from which to choose a potential partner. There were over 2000 growers in the region, which was responsible for almost 42% of the global

Child Labour

In Cote d'Ivoire, Africa, it is estimated that close to 250,000 children work in plantations. 157,000 of those work in the 'worst forms of child labour'. 12,000 of these children are not relatives of the plantation owners, and are suspected to have been trafficked into the country.

In the Democratic Republic of Congo around 40,000 children work in mining.

Around 300,000 children as young as seven are fighting in wars around the world.

2 million children are abused through prostitution and pornography globally. In the UK it is believed that there are 5,000 child prostitutes; 75% of them are girls.

An estimated 8.4 million children are trapped in illegal, degrading and dangerous work, with a total of 218 million children aged 5 – 17 years working as child labourers around the world.

Figures taken from The Small Hands of Slavery, published by Save the Children UK, March 2007

production of cocoa, and Laura knew that focusing her search for a suitable grower in this region was likely to yield her the most success.

Laura remembered that on her previous trip she had been taken to a huge outdoor market where all of the cocoa growers set up stall and sold their wares. After asking around, Laura discovered that what she was looking for was the Daloa cocoa market. Held on Thursdays, this was the place, she was told by locals as she was exploring and familiarizing herself with the area, where she would find what she was looking for; the greatest concentration of cocoa producers in one place at any one time, anywhere in the world. But whilst Laura found such choice exciting and motivating, how was she to know which supplier would be a suitable partner for her ethical endeavours?

&& *It might be the best product in the world, but if you don't like the salesmen you're not going to buy the product.* **&&**

Male aged 68, taken from National Consumer Council study

To say that the market was crowded would be a massive understatement. It was swarming. It was hot. It was dusty. And Laura wasn't happy. Not because of the challenging conditions necessarily; it had more to do with the sheer number of growers, and their pushy approaches. Laura would be within 10 paces of a stall, and she would find herself surrounded by baying children, all pulling at her clothes, dragging her towards 'their' stall, with cries of 'Lady, Lady' in broken, barely coherent English. This was a far cry from the professional and sophisticated world that she was used to. No conference rooms here, no negotiating deals over lunch at swanky restaurants in the West End of London. This was raw and up close, and it wasn't quite what Laura had in mind.

Laura managed to pull herself away from the children of one stall, only to find herself sucked into the vortex created by the children of the next stall in line. It was exhausting and it was heartbreaking. Laura had heard of the way that children as young as six or seven were used in the cocoa industry to pick and carry cocoa beans, but it's one thing to read about it in trade journals, and quite another to experience it first-hand. Laura certainly was experiencing it, and she didn't like it. She didn't like it at all.

Innocent Success
"The Ultimate 21st Century Brand"

In 1998, Richard Reed and his two college friends, Jon and Adam, came up with the idea of setting up a fresh fruit juice company. After six months of developing recipes in their kitchen, the boys wanted to test their drinks with a wider audience. To do so, they bought £500 of fruit, turned it into smoothies and sold them from a stall at a music festival. They put up a sign that said, 'Should we give up our jobs to make these smoothies?', and put out a big bin that said NO and one that said YES. At the end of the weekend, the YES bin was full so they went back to work the next day and resigned.

Since that music festival, innocent drinks has grown from £0 to an anticipted £150 million turnover in its first nine years, and is the UK's fastest growing food and drink company. Innocent has been recognized for its enlightened approach to business, where all members of the team have a share in the company, get taken on snowboarding weekends, and have baby bonuses and travel grants.

With packaging promising consumers that their drinks are 100% natural and free from additives, and a bold promise that they will never use concentrated juices, innocent has created a 'corporate personality' that larger more established businesses can't replicate. 10% of profits go to charity, and their ethical policy states "We sure aren't perfect, but we're trying to do the right thing" proven by being the world's first drinks company to use a 100% recycled plastic bottle.

After a couple of hours of being pushed, pulled, cajoled and hollered at, Laura decided it was time for a break. She found a small stall selling various fresh juices. She bought a refreshingly chilled cup of aloe vera juice and stood by the stall watching the crowd bustling around her, lost for a moment in her thoughts.

Draining her cup, Laura thought she heard something in the crowd. She paused for a moment and stood completely still, straining to hear above the noise of the market, and trying to decipher what she thought she heard above the sound of dogs barking, children shouting, and the small group of African men bartering loudly at the next stall.

Sensing that the source was ahead of her in the market, she took a few tentative steps forward, looking around her in the crowd to see whether she could identify the source.

"Miss Laura?"

Laura smiled – she could hear her name being called clearly now, but couldn't locate the source. "Miss Laura, Miss Laura. Over here!"

Suddenly, Laura could see who was calling her name. She pushed her way through the crowd and over to the stall.

"Miss Laura, I thought it was you! It's Koku Amosu, you remember me?" he asked with a little caution in his voice.

"Yes, of course, Koku!" said Laura, shaking his hand warmly. He had a firm handshake, and the skin of a man who was no stranger to the rigours of manual labour.

Trusted sales people are more effective

Universities and market research firms have conducted numerous studies to determine the most important buying decision factors for people who make significant purchases. In an article featured on http://www.highprobsell.com, Jacques Werth, President of High Probability® Selling, discusses how they gathered as many of those studies as they could find, and did simple correlation analyses to average out the results.

Buying Decision Factors	% of people listing each factor in their top 5
Level of Trust in the Salesperson	87
Level of Respect for the Salesperson	82
Reputation of the Company or Product	76
Features of the Product or Service	71
Quality and Service	58
Price (non-commodity)	16
Like the Salesperson	3

"It is a very busy market day today, yes?"

"Yes — it looks like it — I'm quite exhausted" said Laura laughing.

"What are you doing here? Mr JJ, he send you to buy more beans?"

"Well, no, not exactly, I'm here on my own this time, Koku"

"No Mr Steve?"

"No, no Mr Steve. Just me!"

"Oh, ok. Are you looking for beans, or just looking today?" he asked, surreptitiously moving slightly to the right in an attempt to give Laura a better view of the beans laid out in sacks on his stall.

Laura smiled and stifled a snigger. The fact that Koku had shifted himself to display his wares wasn't lost on her.

"Well, I am looking for some beans actually, but I'm looking for a certain type of bean."

Koku looked puzzled. "You no looking for cocoa bean? This is a cocoa bean market. The biggest."

"I am looking for cocoa beans, Koku, but I'm looking for ethical cocoa beans."

Koku started nodding and smiling when Laura emphasized the word ethical. "Good, Miss Laura. Much has happened with Koku since you were here last trip. Much has happened."

"Oh, really?"

"Oh, yes. What you notice about my stall?" He stood aside and waved his arm across his stall, as if to present it to her. "Go on, what you notice?"

Establishing trustworthiness

1. Ask direct questions which can be answered by 'yes' or 'no'. If you get a long-winded response then start to get suspicious

2. Little in life is perfect. If an explanation, set of benefits or case study about a past success sounds too good to be true, then it probably is

3. Long words, jargon and lots of references to people you've never heard of suggest the other person may be trying to punch above their weight. Ask for clarity; if you don't get it start to doubt

4. Ask questions about detail. An interviewer was suspicious about a candidate who claimed to have worked for a well-known advertising agency. "Remind me, what number on Charlotte Street are their offices?", he asked. The candidate, who had only temped there for a week, couldn't remember

5. Be doubly aware if someone is over-friendly and gives you more compliments than you deserve

From themindgym.com

Laura looked at the stall, puzzled. She could see nothing but sacks of cocoa beans, with cocoa butter laid out in small pots in front of each sack, presumably as a sample of the finished product. "I don't know, Koku – you have cocoa beans just like the other stalls."

Koku did a little dance on the spot out of frustration.

"No, Miss Laura. It is just me here – there are no children! There are no children here to bring you to my stall!"

"Oh yes, that's right. That is important, why?"

"It is important because it show you that I no use children in my fields. That is very important now. I no use children at all. Just men and women pick my cocoa. No children."

Laura nodded her approval. "I worked very hard over the last three years to become an ethical grower." Koku rifled in the pocket of his well-worn jeans and pulled out a scrappy piece of paper that looked as if it had been folded and unfolded many times before. He thrust it excitedly in front of Laura. "Look! I am ethical producer!"

Laura looked at the piece of paper. Sure enough, Koku had received a letter from UNICEF which commended his challenge to the local industry with his refusal to use children in the harvesting, packing or transportation of his crops. "This is good, Koku, this is very good" said Laura, passing the piece of paper back to him. Koku looked at it for a second and smiled, even though he must have read the letter hundreds of times previously.

"I am very proud that I have the bless from UNICEF. It is very important to me that they know I do not use children. And I trade direct with the buyers also, so that I

Trade Imbalance

Amsterdam is the world's busiest cocoa port, and from imports of 250,000 tonnes of beans it can expect to earn over $5bn in export sales.

Meanwhile, from exports of 700,000 tonnes of beans, the Ivory Coast can expect to earn no more than $7bn.

do not deal with no middlemen who steal my money."

"And because you deal direct with the buyers, you can then pay fair wages?" asked Laura.

"Yes, Miss Laura. That is why I have no children on my stall, and why people are always knocking on my door trying to get a job with me on my farm. All the workers, they leave these other farms" he said, pointing to the stalls surrounding his, "and many they come to Koku, because they know that Koku will look after them."

Koku was clearly very proud of his achievement. Laura was pleased for him – since the last time that she had seen Koku, when they first met, he had clearly tried hard to differentiate himself from the other growers and follow a road of integrity.

"I can show you my farm if you like?" asked Koku brightly. "I can provide you beans that are the very best quality, and are not harvested with blood."

Whilst this sounded dramatic, Laura appreciated Koku's sentiment.

"Yes, Koku, I think I would like to see your farm very much indeed" replied Laura smiling broadly.

❝ *Better to trust the man who is frequently in error than one who is never in doubt.* **❞**

Eric Sevareid, broadcast journalist

Koku's farm was everything that he purported it to be. The workers were indeed all adults, and they were cared for. They received a meal every day and had somewhere to shelter from the midday sun. Laura was pleased. After some quality testing of the cocoa beans, and of the resultant cocoa butter that Koku produced from the batch that she had inspected, Laura was satisfied that she had found the fairly traded beans she needed to be able to create her chocolate bar. But not only that; the beans were of the quality she was looking for, at a price that would allow her to reach the mid market that was her target population.

Most importantly, she had found a supplier whom she believed she could really trust.

66 *Under conditions of high trust, problem solving tends to be creative and productive. Under conditions of low trust, problem solving tends to be degenerative and ineffective.* **99**

R.Wayne Boss (1977), Harvard Business Review

Back in England, Laura had misjudged exactly how much technical expertise was involved in creating the perfect recipe for a chocolate bar. Finding an ethical producer to supply her with the raw materials was just the first step. Now she was faced with a whole host of different challenges, not least of which was having no access to the Research & Development expertise and facilities that she was used to at Gabriels.

Undeterred, Laura dipped into her little black book.

Sarah Clutch had been quite the rising star at Gabriels. Despite joining Gabriels just a few years ago, Sarah already had a significant amount of success under her belt. Tinkering away in the corner of their research kitchen, in between her 'real' work of product and quality testing Gabriels' products, she had created the Mallow Pillow, a chocolate bar which was wider than other bars and was produced to look just like a pillow – hence the name, and consisted of soft, fluffy marshmallow smothered in milk chocolate. It was irresistibly delicious and had become a best seller from the moment it had hit the shelves. Achieving such breakthrough success so early in her career meant that she had caught JJ's eye and, as such, had met Laura at the many

Trust Increases Innovation

If innovation often leads to success, why do businesses struggle to achieve it?

This is a question of trust. Distrust makes employees unhappy, uncooperative, and guarded, whereas trust catalyzes creativity, critical thinking, and collaboration.

If distrust is the norm in your organization, it may be due to managers lacking the skills to establish "transactional" trust: Reina & Reina (1999) describe "transactional trust" as involving others in decision-making; managing expectations and delegating appropriately; and telling the truth, sharing information, and speaking with integrity. Businesses also need to build what these authors call "transformational" trust through relationship-based management practices. Even "unintentional minor betrayals," such as gossip and backbiting, weaken trust and undermine workers' initiative, commitment, and willingness to share knowledge.

From the book "Trust and Betrayal in the Workplace: Building Effective Relationships in Your Organization" (Berrett-Koehler, 1999), Dennis S. Reina and Michelle L. Reina.

lunches and events that JJ held for his small band of hand-picked protégées.

Being around the same age and from similar backgrounds, the two girls had bonded and had become quite a force to be reckoned with in the company. Needless to say, when Sarah, who had left Gabriels around the same time as Laura in order to devote herself to raising her young family, received a call from an excited Laura out of the blue, she was genuinely pleased to hear from her friend. Despite motherhood giving her the fulfilment she had been looking for, she did miss the excitement and creativity of her past life at Gabriels.

There was something in Laura's voice that compelled Sarah to listen. And listen she did, as Laura recounted her experience and adventures since leaving Gabriels. She was intrigued by Laura's description of her awakening to the importance of trust and integrity in her approach to business. Sarah was amazed that such an important notion could disappear from anyone's radar, it being so central to her own.

66 *Creativity comes from trust. Trust your instincts. And never hope more than you work.* 99

Rita Mae Brown, author

"Ok, try this" said Sarah, passing a pale blue mixing bowl over to Laura, disturbing her focus on the figures that she was scribbling on the pad in front of her.

The kitchen table in Laura's flat was covered with bars of chocolate, bags of sugar and various bottles and packets of exotic flavourings. Sarah looked exhausted and her apron, stained with chocolate and dusted with sugar, would suggest to any observer that the two friends had clearly been experimenting in the cramped kitchen of Laura's flat for some time.

"Yep, that's good, that's good, but the flavour isn't strong enough yet. The colour also looks a little pale – can you make it a deeper brown? Kind of in between the colour of traditional milk and plain chocolate? I want people to see the difference as well as taste it."

Laura had no idea how difficult that might be for Sarah, only that she had a clear idea in her mind of what her end product should look like. And that wasn't it.

Sarah brushed her fringe away with the back of her hand, smudging a little chocolate onto her forehead, and sighed gently. "You got it, boss!" she joked.

66 *The leaders who work most effectively, it seems to me, never say 'I'. And that's not because they have trained themselves not to say 'I.' They don't think 'I.' They think 'we'; they think 'team.' They understand their job to be to make the team function. They accept responsibility and don't sidestep it, but 'we' gets the credit…This is what creates trust, what enables you to get the task done.* **99**

Peter Drucker, writer and management consultant

"That's it! That's just what I was looking for – perfect!" Laura was ecstatic. The weeks and weeks of experimenting had paid off. Thanks to Sarah, she had the taste that she was looking for. The chocolate was a deep brown colour. Sarah had somehow managed to give it a delightfully creamy flavour, with a hint of vanilla and ginger, which gave the chocolate a light, yet luxurious taste to it.

"You know" said Sarah, "quite apart from the ethical angle, we've created a winner here. The taste is unusual, yet compelling, and the texture is great – it's like liquid velvet. You've got a success on your hands with this one, Laura."

Laura smiled, a smile that suggested she was happy, proud, and comfortable with her achievement; but there was none of the arrogance that there once would have been when she had received feedback like that. "Thanks, Sarah. It's a joint effort – we did it together. I couldn't have done this on my own."

Sarah nodded in response. "So, what now? Have you thought about what you're going to call it?"

Laura smiled, a glint in her eye. "Oh yes. After the journey that I've been through over the last few months, I wanted a name that captures the lessons that I've learned through all of this, that encapsulates the importance of the trust and

Brand image v brand trust

A brand is more than a product itself. Companies should spend effort in creating and informing consumers about the correct attitudes and behaviours of their brand. The relationship between a brand and its consumers has become increasingly complex in recent years as consumers have easy access to more knowledge than they used to, and the internet allows for straightforward comparisons between brands.

Brand trust is one element of brand image since trust is a vital ingredient in generating an intense bond between the consumer and the brand.

Analysis of the brand associations made by consumers will inform the marketing of a brand's image with the goal of increasing brand trust and evoking positive emotional reaction to the brand.

Brand associations fall into three categories:
1. Attributes
2. Benefits
3. Attitudes

integrity that I had chosen to ignore in my quest for my personal gain and success. I've realised that integrity and trust are the crucial ingredients for success in any walk of life. So, I think there's only one name that this bar, and all that it represents, deserves."

"What's that?" asked Sarah, with obvious curiosity.

"*true.*"

Sarah considered the name for a second. "Perfect!"

66 *Trust each other again and again. When the trust level gets high enough, people transcend apparent limits, discovering new and awesome abilities of which they were previously unaware.* 99

David Armistead, author

Laura was deadset in her mind from the moment that she had come up with the name that there was only one possible design for her chocolate bar. And so it was: a deep brown chocolate bar with the imprint of an angel's wing on each chunk, enclosed within matt silver paper, and wrapped in a pure white sleeve. The silver lettering on the wrapper spelled out the word *true*, in beautiful calligraphy, with the words 'indulgence for the conscience' underneath.

When Laura saw the prototype for the first time, she was overcome with emotion. This had long been a dream for her, and to hold the finished product, the product of her journey of self-awakening, in her hand was emotional. *true* did look amazing – it made a quietly confident statement that would place it in a league of its own amongst the other bars on the shelves, which largely relied on lurid colour and exclamation marks to get the consumers' attention. *true* was elegant, self-assured, ethical and quite, quite delicious.

There was one person that Laura was desperate to share her achievement with. She made her way to Steve's delicatessen, and was amazed to see that there was a queue to get in! She looked through the window, and sure enough, Steve and William were run ragged inside the deli, trying to

How Brands Connect

Advertising is used to connect a brand or product with its consumers in order to create sustainable advantage. The most common failures in advertising campaigns lie in misjudging the emotional needs of the consumer.

According to Inside Research newsletter, $117 billion was spent in 2002 on advertising in the U.S., and $6.8 billion spent on things such as focus groups, opinion polls and ad and market tracking (Wells 2003).

Studies into failing brands have proved that it is more important to know why consumers are motivated to buy than it is to know how many people prefer one product attribute to another. Researchers have also proved that people are emotionally similar, and that people do not buy products or behave socially because of their demographics, but because of the way things make them feel.

Well, M. (2003) In Search of the Buy Button. Forbes, Sept 1, 2003. pp 62-70
www.brandtrust.com

get through the queue of customers. Laura stopped and watched them both in action for a while. Despite being very busy, and obviously keen to serve everyone waiting as quickly and efficiently as possible, Laura couldn't help but notice that the two guys had a smile for everyone. Some of the shoppers with time on their hands clearly wanted to chat, and so they bantered while they were pulling together their order. Laura was impressed. She made her way to the end of the queue and waited patiently. As she did so, inching slowly to the front of the queue, she reflected on how her behaviour had changed. It wouldn't have been so long ago that the Laura of old would have pushed her way to the front of the queue and used her relationship with Steve to do so, but instead, Laura waited her turn like everyone else.

Steve was cleaning up from serving his last customer when Laura reached the counter.

"And what can I get... Laura!"

Steve bustled round the counter and gave his friend a big hug. "You look great – how are you doing?"

Before Laura could answer, Steve looked behind her and saw that the queue had dissipated to almost nothing, and signalled to William. "Will, can you look after these people for me?"

"Sure thing!"

And with that, Steve led Laura into the back of the delicatessen. They stood amongst boxes of olive oil and hams hanging from the ceiling, whilst Steve reached into

Don't trust the label

In the food industry, the packaging label plays an important role in conveying information to its consumers. An international survey carried out by nine leading consumer organisations investigated how consumers can tell which labels are trustworthy, and what the effects are when consumers are misled. Focussing on 'green claims', the aim was to see whether labels displaying green credentials were actually produced in a sustainable way. The report claims that a large number of different logos and claims are vague, meaningless and non-transparent, lacking standards and third party verification. 12 recommendations are made, with the most important message being that to evoke consumer trust, labels and claims on food should be clear and unambiguous, and that they should all be developed with stakeholder involvement and be publicly available, open and accessible so that consumers can be sure of their validity.

the fridge for some pressed apple juice.

"Looks like things are going very well for you here, Steve? You've got people literally queuing out the door!"

"I know, it's amazing! Since we last met, things have taken off and we are doing really well – there's a queue most afternoons. We're getting to know most of the regulars, and building up quite a reputation in the locale, so it's all working out quite nicely."

"So, you're glad you quit Gabriels, then?"

"Oh, without a doubt. Don't get me wrong, this is jolly hard work, but much more satisfying. I'd wanted to run a delicatessen for so long; I'm finding it exhausting, but so rewarding. It's what I always wanted to do. It's great – I'm really being true to myself."

Laura laughed, and then caught herself and put her hand over her mouth, realising how this might appear to Steve.

"What? What are you laughing for?"

"Sorry, Steve, you must think me rude. I'm not laughing at you. It's just your turn of phrase. It's spooky."

Steve was still none the wiser and it showed on his face.

Laura reached into her bag and brought out a small cardboard box. Without a word, she placed the box on the table and, opening it up, she reached inside and pulled out one of her chocolate bars. She held it in the palm of her hand and offered it to him as if it was a precious jewel.

Reading the name of the chocolate bar, Steve looked at Laura and laughed. Intrigued, Steve picked up the bar. "What's this?"

Laura smiled. "You remember when I was here the last

Trusted Marks

Emotions triggered from the first sight of a logo have to be positive and ideally encourage trust among consumers. The Kitemark has been a registered symbol for over a hundred years and is an excellent example of a recognised mark of trust and respected brand values.

According to the GfK NOP Consumer Survey 2006, the Kitemark was recognisable to 82% of those consumers asked. More importantly, 80% of the 1,000 respondents stated they would put more trust in a product carrying the Kitemark since it would represent higher quality than other products, and would make them more likely to make a purchase.

time and we talked about the importance of trust, respect, authenticity and all that stuff in business?"

"Sure. May I?" asked Steve as he opened the wrapping and snapped off a chunk of chocolate.

"Go ahead. Well, after meeting up with Otis, it just got me to thinking that that was what I was missing. The notion of trust. I had lost sight of that completely. So, I decided that I would put that right before it was too late. Being fired from Gabriels was a real wake up call, Steve. So, I decided to do what JJ had originally charged me with, partly, I think, to prove to myself that it could be done."

"Mmmm, this is really good, really good. What could be done?"

Laura rolled her eyes. "The Fairtrade chocolate bar, Steve!"

"Of course, I'm only kidding. So how did you do it?"

Over the apple juice and some of the finest carrot cake, just delivered by a local amateur baker, Laura shared the story with her friend of how she travelled to Africa, sourced the beans, and worked with Sarah, amongst others, to bring *true* to life.

Steve was impressed. "You've done well, Laura. I'm pleased to see that you have learned the most important lesson in business, if not in life. And the name, *true*, says it all. I love it."

Endorsement such as this from someone whom she respected so much was important to Laura, and made her feel secure that she had done the right thing. Chased the right dream. Backed the right horse.

World's Richest Man Does Deals On Trust

Investment genius Warren Buffett became the world's richest man, according to Forbes in March 2008. Known for a desire to act decisively, and often on a handshake, he exemplifies the wisdom of valuing trust. In October 1999, Barry & Eliot Tatleman sold their Jordans furniture business to Warren Buffett's Berkshire Hathaway for a rumoured cash sum of $250 million. Buffett, who likes to keep existing management in place when he buys a business, reportedly did the deal that the two brothers would stay on without a signed agreement - particularly brave given that Jordans is famed for its TV commercials fronted by the two brothers. When Barry Tatleman was asked why Buffett had taken them at their word, he told a reporter "It's a new concept in business. It's called trust."

"In fact" said Steve, pausing, "how about we give it a go here?"

Laura wasn't quite sure what her friend meant. "Huh?"

"Well, why don't we stock it here in the deli and see how it does? I'll certainly vouch for it – it looks great, and it tastes delicious. And it's ethical. What's not to like?"

"Wow, that's wonderful! But I didn't come here to convince you to stock it!" said Laura, a little embarrassed.

"I know, and that's one of the reasons why I want to, Laura. It didn't even cross your mind, did it?"

"No, not at all."

"Right – but it would have been at the forefront of the old Laura's mind!" said Steve, nudging Laura playfully with his elbow.

Laura smiled "Yes, probably!"

The two friends shook on the deal. Steve would trial selling *true* in his deli, and agreed that Laura would bring over some boxes of her pride and joy the next day for him to display on the counter tops.

After hand-packing the few remaining bars that she and Sarah had produced in the prototype batch, Laura did just that, praying all the way to the delicatessen the next day that the product of her ethical rehabilitation would be a success.

66 *Trust in God but lock your car.* **99**

H. Jackson Brown, Jr

The following afternoon, Laura was poring over a production spreadsheet fantasising about the success which she dreamed of for her progeny, when her mobile rang.

"Laura, hi, it's Steve."

"Hello Steve, how are you? Have you sold any of my chocolate bars yet?"

"Sold any? They've flown out, Laura! In fact, they've all gone! I was calling to see how quickly you could come round with some more."

Laura was dumbfounded. Her hand floated away from her ear as she took a moment to process what Steve had said to her.

"Laura? Laura? Are you there?"

"What? Oh yes, I'm here, Steve, I'm here. Wow, that's amazing. Let me see what I can do."

66 In the era that lies ahead, the trusted business man, the prudent fiduciary and the honest steward must again be the paradigms of our great American enterprises. 99

John C. Bogle, Founder and former CEO of Vanguard Mutual, in his book The Battle for the Soul of Capitalism, 2005 Yale University Press

It wasn't long before there were other shop owners who were calling Laura. The reputation of *true* had spread fast. It seemed that the idea of a delicious, ethical, reasonably priced alternative to the standard chocolate bars on the shelves was an untapped market. And a pretty popular one at that. Laura was delighted. Production of *true* had quickly outgrown her kitchen table, and she was loving spending her time finding a production facility that could produce the quantities that had been nothing but a fantasy just a short time ago. Laura had surprised a number of the owners of small factories when, after the tour of their production areas, she had asked to see the rest areas that were in place for workers and enquired about pay rates and employee benefits. Laura was enjoying the unexpected scale of her success and revelling in her new approach. She felt alive, refreshed. She felt true to herself.

Laura had been featured in the local newspaper after one of their journalists picked up *true* when they stopped in Steve's delicatessen for lunch one day. He so enjoyed the bar and the story behind it (which he had learnt from Steve, who had become Laura's biggest advocate) that he wrote an article about Laura and *true,* which had increased her local exposure still further. As a consequence, her mobile

EQ (Emotional Intelligence Quotient)

EQ is a combination of competencies that contribute to a person's ability to manage and monitor his or her own emotions, to correctly gauge the emotional state of others, and to influence opinions. Daniel Goleman highlights 5 components:

1. Self awareness
2. Self management
3. Motivation
4. Empathy
5. Social skills

Emotional Intelligence by Daniel Goleman 1995

Trustworthiness is an essential part of emotional maturity. If people do not trust you, you may have to justify every detail of every decision. Trust helps people to get on with their lives, and is essential for innovation and creativity. Trust can take years to build and seconds to destroy. The consequences of abused trust can hurt an organisation, a family, or a friendship.

phone seemingly never stopped ringing. However, there was one call that she never expected to receive.

"Hello? Is that Laura Anderson?"

"Yes?"

"Laura Anderson, local hero?"

"Well, I don't know about that! Who is this?"

"Oh come now Laura, don't you recognise my voice?"

In that moment, Laura did. It couldn't be, could it?

"JJ?"

"The very same. How are you, my dear? I've heard all about you and your chocolate bar. Couldn't resist having a nibble myself, actually. Splendid taste. A hint of ginger, I think?"

"Oh, you've tasted it?" said Laura, surprised at the level of interest JJ appeared to be taking in her endeavours.

"Oh yes, yes, indeed. I really like it. It's really quite good."

"Well, thank you, JJ, I appreciate that." She hadn't spoken with JJ since he unceremoniously fired her during the Board meeting, and she didn't particularly want to rake over that incident again with him. Why was he calling?

"I was very disappointed when you had to leave us, Laura."

'Had to leave us?' What is he talking about – he fired me! she thought. JJ's turn of phrase had riled Laura, although she tried not to let it seep into her tone of voice.

"Not half as sorry as I was, I can assure you!" Laura replied, in an effort to steer the conversation away from her past misdemeanours.

Trust in the Workplace

Development Dimensions International (DDI) conducted a Study of Trust in the Workplace. DDI surveyed 1,108 people from 57 organisations considered to be representative of U.S. organisations as a whole. Their findings are summarised below:

- Of the four groups rated (peers, leaders, other teams, senior management) respondents were most likely to trust their leaders and least likely to trust senior management

- Approximately half the respondents viewed lack of trust as a problem in their organisation

- Organisational position, job tenure, industry type and company size did not affect ratings of trust, indicating that trust issues are not related to company demographics

- Important behaviours associated with trusted leaders were: consistent behaviour, dependability/reliability, support during risk taking, and keeping people's best interests in mind

"I had great plans for you, Laura, and I was genuinely very fond of you – you do know that don't you?"

"Yes, yes, I do. I know I let you down, JJ" she replied thoughtfully.

"Well, we all make mistakes, my dear. But I didn't call you to talk about the past – that's over and done with. We can only hope to learn from our mistakes and look to the future. I'm not impervious to the odd lapse of judgement now and again you know, we're all human."

Laura was comforted by his generosity. She had given herself a hard time since her magnificent error of judgement at Gabriels, and it was really only since her trip to Africa that she had begun to allow herself to think that she was truly correcting the errors she had made in her personal behaviour and integrity.

"Which brings me to why I wanted to give you a call. You see, I have a confession to make. The Fairtrade project I gave you was a little bit of a test, a challenge, your own little odyssey if you will."

"Right" said Laura nervously. She didn't know what was coming next, only that with JJ, anything was possible.

He continued. "I wasn't sure that creating a Fairtrade bar as a real alternative to the myriad of chocolate bars on the market today was actually a possibility. I wasn't sure that it could be done. And, judging from your proposals in the Boardroom that day, after all your research you confirmed my suspicions."

Laura was confused. "So, if you pretty much knew that it couldn't be done, why did you fire me?"

Top 5 least trusted professions

Profession	% responding 'trusted a great deal/quite a lot'
1. Politicians	7%
2. Car Salesmen	17%
3. Trade Union Leaders	23%
4. Football Players	24%
5. Journalists	29%

Results from the 2007 Readers Digest Trusted Brands Survey of over 24,000 residents of Europe

"Well, you confirmed my suspicions, yes. But I fully expected you to come to that conclusion and no more. Not for one minute could I predict that you had become so focused on your ambition to the exclusivity of everything else that you would not only throw your own ethics out of the window, but also those of my family firm, and suggest that we lie to our customers. That was why I fired you." Laura picked up a trace of resurfacing anger in JJ's voice.

"Yes, that wasn't my greatest moment."

"You were one of my best people, Laura, and I knew that if you decided that it couldn't be done, then it really couldn't." Uncharacteristically, JJ paused for a moment. "But, you were always determined and you didn't let it go, did you? You couldn't let it beat you. And you have, against all the odds, found a way to make it happen. But not just to make it happen, Laura – you have really created something very special here. The taste, the design of the packaging, the name. It's all so perfectly fluent. It's compelling."

Laura was taken aback with the extent of JJ's praise. "Thank you" she said quietly.

There was a moment of silence between them. Laura waited for her old boss to speak. Had he made the point that he called to make? Was this a simple congratulatory phone call? As JJ continued, it would seem not. "You know, we would love to have this product in our portfolio, Laura." Laura stood, dumbfounded. What was JJ saying? Was he offering her her job back?

"I don't understand."

"Well, quite simply, I love what you have done with *true*,

Trust and the Plumber

Charles Handy, the writer and the man many refer to as the first business guru, spent a period of his career as one of BBC Radio 4's contributors to Thought for the Day. On one occasion, he shared this thought on the subject of trust and forgiveness:

"My problems with my plumber may sound trivial but they may be clues to the world we live in; a barometer on the weather ahead. He's a nice chap my plumber, and I trust him. So when we agreed a price to fit an outside tap, I thought that was that.

He fixed the tap, but instead of putting it above the gulley where drips would wash away, he put it 3 feet to the left where it would slop all over the grass, making a muddy puddle. When I complained, he said "It's against water board regulations to put a tap over a drain."

My wife checked this out and it transpired he was lying to get himself out of a corner. I forgave him because I wanted him to sort it out and he did, reluctantly.

I seem to have been required to forgive an awful lot of people lately for broken promises, missed deadlines, bad work or lost money. People who I trusted but who let me down.

No relationship can survive and grow unless we are prepared to trust and forgive when the trust goes wrong, again and again and again. No forgiveness means no relationship."

I believe that you have created something really special here and, let's be honest, my dear, without access to Gabriels vast manufacturing capability you would never really be able to take *true* to the audience that it deserves by operating as a little cottage industry. This could be wildly successful. Listen, we have a Board meeting tomorrow, why don't you come in and see us all, present *true* to the Board, and we'll talk it over? You know it makes sense – it's a waste to have this great achievement of yours only enjoyed by a small, local audience."

She knew that JJ had a point, and Laura recognised that she would be going full circle if she could win the Board over with *true*.

JJ's offer was such an opportunity, that she didn't take long to consider her response.

"Ok, yes, ok, let's do it!"

"Splendid, splendid. We are meeting at 10am tomorrow morning – why don't you pop along then? It will be lovely to see you again, Laura."

Laura prepared herself for the unexpected meeting the next day. In days gone by, an offer like this would have seen her instantly become a swirl of activity, rushing around and working into the small hours to pull together an all singing and dancing PowerPoint presentation for her meeting with the big cheeses the following day. Instead, Laura boiled the kettle, made herself a mug of tea, and reflected on the call that she had just received. This was certainly a turn up for the books. She was pleased that JJ knew what she had achieved since leaving his employ,

Hidden Barriers to Trust

1. Distance Barriers – much communication in business lacks physical presence (for example telephone, email) giving rise to psychological separation

2. Physical Barriers – the structure of the meeting place

3. Language Barriers – the language used may not be the first language of both parties

4. Cultural Barriers – trust may mean different things and be built in different ways

and thrilled that a man so prevalent and respected within the chocolate and confectionery industry would give her creation such a glowing report. So glowing, in fact, that he sounded like he wanted to include it within his own stable of products. That was quite an honour. Ironically, thought Laura, the opportunity that appeared to be in the offing was the kind of success that she had always dreamed about, and she found it intriguing that she was not experiencing the grasping, delirious excitement that she would have felt before her fall from grace and her subsequent reawakening to what was truly important in life.

" *We do not believe in ourselves until someone reveals that deep inside us is valuable, worth listening to, worthy of our trust, sacred to our touch. Once we believe in ourselves, we can risk curiosity, wonder, spontaneous delight or any experience that reveals the human spirit.* "

E.E. Cummings, poet

JJ had obviously done a 'sell job' on the Board because when Laura walked into the imposing Boardroom, she did not receive the negative vibes that she was anticipating. Instead, there was hand shaking, warm smiles, and cries of "good to have you back." It appeared that Laura's past misdemeanours had been forgiven, or at the very least, forgotten. But Laura was politically savvy enough to know that this warm welcome may not have been entirely authentic – JJ had made it clear that he wanted *true* as a Gabriels product, and it was in his and the Board's interest to make Laura feel as comfortable and valued as possible. Despite that, Laura did feel a sense of closure being back at Gabriels, back at the scene of the crime, as it were, and receiving a more positive response than the one that accompanied the last presentation she had made to this group.

Laura chose not to take the traditional and well-trodden route of PowerPoint to get her message across, instead opting for a more personal approach. She told the Board about her excitement of joining Gabriels, of how her ambition had changed her during her climb up the corporate ladder, and how she had lost touch with her integrity, which had resulted in her unceremonious sacking within this very room. Laura couldn't help but notice some members of

The Power of the Story

Story-telling is a time-tested way of establishing trust and rapport. A story does what facts and figures never can; it evokes emotion, it inspires, and it motivates. Telling the story behind the business is an opportunity to build an emotional bond with the audience, as well as conveying complex information in a succinct manner.

Some key components of storytelling are:
- Loading stories with key emotional ingredients
- Delivering core messages clearly and powerfully for lasting impact
- Motivating your audience to support your goals
- Strengthening company culture through use of stories
- Displaying the authentic personality of the leaders to inspire loyalty
- Injecting energy and passion into the campaign

the Board shifting uncomfortably in their seats when she recounted that particular part of her journey. She explained how, quite by accident, she had bumped into Steve who had been on a similar journey and was now running a very successful delicatessen. She told the story of Otis and his pink, spiky haired waiter, and the charging system that operated solely on trust. She threw a stack of photographs onto the long Boardroom table as she talked about her journey to Africa, which enabled her to later create *true* literally at her kitchen table.

Emphasising her personal journey and the learning she made at each stage of her story, Laura explained how *true* was the physical manifestation of her personal reawakening to those things that are easily lost sight of in the corporate world: trust, ethics, and a sense of integrity. Again, there was embarrassed shuffling around the table. Perhaps Laura's story was hitting home with some of the people sitting around the table who may not have always kept these factors at the forefront of their minds when building their own careers.

Laura finished by walking around the long table and giving each Board member an opportunity to sample the results of her very personal journey. The murmurs of chocolate fuelled pleasure spoke for themselves.

JJ took the floor in typical flamboyant fashion.
"Impressive, Laura, and I mean that in every sense of the word. I am sure that I speak for everyone here when I

Selection-Attraction-Attrition Model

The organisational culture and climate of your organisation is influenced by every person associated with it. Schneider & Reichers (1983) proposed the Selection-Attraction-Attrition Model which suggests that people are attracted to organisations that they anticipate will, in some way, match their personalities or self-concepts. In the same way, organisations try hard to attract people who will fit in well with their working environment and their values.

say that it was very difficult for us to let you go…"; the members of the Board nodded in agreement. Laura thought she even heard a "hear, hear" in the mêlée of mumbling "…but it appears that you have turned this situation around in the most impressive way. You have been on a tremendous personal journey, and one that has brought about an outstanding product."

Signalling the end of his soliloquy, JJ turned towards the Board who responded with a rousing round of applause.

"Now, to business. As a Board, we've been looking for a way to break into the 'green' market for quite some time. We know that this is something that's becoming increasingly important to our customers, which is why I set you off on the task to see whether it could be done." Laura thought it curious that JJ was talking as if she had never left. She listened as he continued.

"I know I speak for all of us when I say that we have been so impressed with not only what you have achieved with *true*, but also your personal epiphanies along the way, that I would like to offer you the opportunity to come back and join us at Gabriels. But this time, Laura" JJ paused dramatically, "as Head of Products."

To say Laura was taken aback was an understatement. She stood for a moment and attempted to process what JJ had just said to her. To be given the opportunity to be welcomed back into the Gabriels fold was one thing. The fact that she had been offered the position of Head of Products was positively overwhelming. This was the golden ticket, the job that Laura (and most other people

3 simple steps for trust building

1. Never make promises that you are not able, or are not intending to keep

2. Never ask others to do anything that you would not do yourself

3. Ensure your people know that they can count on your respect and your loyalty, unless and until they prove undeserving

Remember that trust is mutual, so by demonstrating that you have trust in your staff, you will prove to them you are worthy of trust yourself.

that joined the company in any branding or product-related job) had her sights on from the very beginning of her career at Gabriels. This was the job that controlled the entire product catalogue and range – past, present, and future. It was a job of tremendous responsibility and recognition, not to mention power. The future of household brands, brands that she had grown up with, would all be in Laura's hands. It was all she had ever wanted. And it was within her grasp.

The room was quiet enough to hear a pin drop. Everyone looked at Laura, awaiting her reaction.

Laura, however, consumed by her own thoughts, was oblivious to the attention. She turned towards the huge floor to ceiling window and looked down onto the Gabriels plant below, watching the workers bustle about. One day soon, *true* could be one of the products that's made down there, she thought, rolling off those production lines. That lorry could be full of my chocolate bars being driven to the farthest reaches of the country and, perhaps one day, the world. The very real possibility of global domination made Laura smile.

66 *Great things are not done by impulse, but by a series of small things brought together.* **99**

Vincent Van Gogh

Today had been particularly busy for Steve at the deli. The queue had again been snaking out of the door for most of the day, and he and William collapsed onto a couple of patio chairs just as soon as they brought them into the shop after another exhausting day.

"You know what, Will, I don't think we can cope with this level of demand for much longer, do you?"

"I tell you, I've never worked as hard in my life!" replied his assistant, exhaling as he stretched his legs out in front of him and put his hands behind his head.

"I think it's time we thought about expanding. There's a unit that's become available on the other side of town that might be worth looking at, and that would give us exposure on both sides of town. It'll give us a big catchment area, save some of our customers from travelling, and also give us an opportunity to broaden our reach somewhat."

"Good idea – maybe we could even start selling more local organic produce - there are a few really big farms over that way."

"Right – that would give people a real alternative to the supermarkets. Yeah, I like it – I'll look into that tomorrow."

Trust can reduce stress

When people fail to trust colleagues, they have a tendency to:

- Attend unnecessary meetings in case people talk behind their back
- Request to be copied in on unnecessary emails
- Fail to delegate
- Experience anxiety that they may be passed over for promotion
- Conclude that when things don't go their way that a plot exists against them
- Not ask for help in case they are seen as weak

"Only thing is though, with my wife about to have the baby, I wouldn't be able to make it over there every day – that's an extra half an hour, and I'm going to be needed at home, mate."

"Mmmm, I hadn't thought of that. I don't fancy rushing between two delis either, to be honest. That's not going to go down well at home either" said Steve, rolling his eyes. William laughed. They both knew that one of the reasons Steve had left Gabriels was to give himself a better work-life balance, so that he could spend more time with his family while they were growing up. Getting back into the long hours that he had felt obliged to chalk up when he was in full-time employment didn't interest Steve, and certainly wouldn't please his wife. Yet he had discovered such a winning formula with the delicatessen, Steve knew that there was a golden opportunity here that was his for the taking. He was torn.

Just at that moment, Steve's eyes came to rest on the box of *true* bars sitting on top of the counter. It made him think for a moment.

"You know what? I think I might just have a solution. Pass me the phone, Will."

66 *Success is not the key to happiness. Happiness is the key to success. If you love what you are doing, you will be successful.* **99**

Albert Schweitzer, winner 1952 Nobel Peace Prize

Laura turned to face the Board. They were on tenterhooks. She stood in silence and smiled. The Board members all looked at each other with self-congratulatory smiles. JJ gave Laura his trademark wink.

"Thank you, but no thanks."

The jovial atmosphere turned on a sixpence. The Board took a collective intake of breath, and they all looked to JJ. "I'm sorry – what do you mean, no thanks?" boomed JJ. "I really appreciate your offer. I really do, and it wasn't so long ago that I would have bitten your hand off at an offer like that. Being Head of Products was all I ever wanted. But, you know, it's not any more. Leaving here broke my heart, but in many ways it was one of the best things that ever happened to me. Following that path, I had lost sight of who I was, and what was really important. My sense of integrity, of doing the right thing, had disappeared. Well, now I'm making some changes. I've rediscovered the Laura I used to be before I got wrapped up in sales figures and promotions. I'm rediscovering the importance of taking action because it's the right thing to do, not because it's the most profitable. Of being truthful, being ethical, being true." Laura emphasised the last word with a passion that

Savings from outsourcing require trust

Research carried out across 450 organisations by Warwick Business School in 2005 found that well-managed outsourcing arrangements based on mutual trust could create a 20% to 40% difference on service, quality, cost and other performance indicators over outdated power-based relationships. The study showed that CEOs who neglect to actively manage their relationships with outsourcing partners are missing out on a 'trust dividend' worth up to 40% of the total contract value.

wasn't lost on those sitting around the long Board table.

JJ looked at Laura with a mixture of frustration and disbelief. This wasn't the response that he was expecting, not at all. He had assumed that Laura would jump at being handed such an opportunity. In that moment, he quickly came to realise that he had significantly underestimated this young woman.

His protegée had risen like a majestic phoenix from the ashes of her career, and it was her level of courage and principle that had truly impressed. And very few people had the capacity to impress JJ Gabriel. But, against all the odds, Laura had.

JJ surprised himself as much as his Board, who sat in stunned confusion, with his response.

"Well, if you won't join us, what will happen to *true*?" asked JJ.

Laura took a deep breath and looked each of the Directors in the eye, finally focussing on JJ. "*true* represents who I have become" she said thoughtfully.

"So you are content to see your creation fade into obscurity are you Laura?" JJ couldn't help himself.

"If it came to it, yes. But there is another way."

She had attracted the Board's attention.

"When I was in Africa I met up with a man called Koku Amosu; in fact, he farms the beans that go into *true*. His approach to farming is radically different; rather than exploiting children from across the border in Mali as the

Cloned Cocoa

It's believed that a leading UK chocolate manufacturer has patented two genes thought to be responsible for the taste of high quality West African Amelonado cocoa. These genes could be transferred into lower quality, higher yielding and cheaper varieties of cocoa, creating the impression of quality. Cocoa traders and retailers would save huge amounts of money by not paying the premium attached to the high quality cocoa, thus depriving cocoa farmers of their livelihood.

other farms do, he's employing local adults for a fair wage, with excellent conditions. He's proved that cocoa can be produced ethically".

"That's all very well but how does it get *true* onto the nation's shelves?" asked JJ.

The young woman, centre stage in the imposing Boardroom took a deep breath. "I'll allow you to produce and market *true*" proposed Laura, "on the condition that you immediately introduce an ethical sourcing policy that ensures that no forced labour is used in the harvest of cocoa, that all of the farmers are paid a fair price for their cocoa beans, and not just for *true*, but for all of the chocolate that Gabriels produce".

"That's an enormous condition" retorted JJ. "You are asking us to turn the cocoa market on its head. It will cause chaos; I think that risk is too great".

For the first time, another director spoke up. "Of course it's risky, JJ, but as I see it, if we don't take a stand now in a few years we'll find ourselves in greater trouble. The consumer is becoming increasingly interested in where their food comes from – this could be as big as the genetically modified crops debate! This could be our opportunity to become a leader in this field, rather than as a follower."

"I agree" came another voice from across the Boardroom. Before long, the entire Board had joined in a chorus of support for this new approach.

Finally, JJ could take no more, and he rose to his feet to take the floor.

Pharmaceutical Giants Give Away Products

Merck, the American pharmaceutical business, discovered that their product Mectizan developed to treat parasitic diseases in animals such as horses could also cure a condition called onchocerciasis in humans. More commonly known as river blindness, this tropical disease affects 18 million people worldwide, particularly in developing countries. In 1987, Merck committed to provide Mectizan free of charge to anyone that needed it, for as long as they needed it.

Twenty years on, this commitment is estimated to represent a value of $2.7 billion and has inspired other drug companies to make similar gestures. In 2007, Pfizer donated antibiotics to treat 60 million trachoma sufferers, GlaxoSmithKline contributed 150 million tablets to treat elephantiasis, Novartis donations helped to cure over 4 million people of leprosy, and Sanofi-Aventis, along with Bayer, gave away medications for sleeping sickness.

These acts of kindness may well be motivated in part by a desire to generate good publicity, but the impact goes much further. The US government, the United Nations and the World Health Organisation have all made commitments to tackle neglected tropical diseases including river blindness that infect a billion people resulting in a million deaths. When challenged on why a profit making organisation would be involved in such a venture, Merck's Ken Gustaven said "We do it because (and people don't like to believe this) it's the right thing to do."

"Ok, I submit. This company was built on taking the initiative – let's go away, look at the numbers, and find a way to make this happen".

JJ turned to Laura, and with a discrete and heartfelt bow of his head, continued. "Thank you, Laura. Once again, you have stirred up emotion in this Boardroom, but this time the impact could reach way beyond those gathered here today. This could be the moment when we chose to do something quite spectacular".

Spontaneous applause from the assembled Board filled the room, which Laura accepted gracefully, more than a little proud of the change that her very personal journey had facilitated.

66 *The Quakers believed that when you lived so that your character matters more to you than success, you discover that people trust you. Bosses will trust you, as will those who work for you. Even some customers will trust you! And, in the long run, trust pays dividends. They may not be as large as if you'd manipulated, lied and short-changed others – but they will be sweeter.* 99

Rob Parsons in The Heart of Success, Hodder & Stoughton

Laura traipsed through the Farmers Market, her Wellington boots attracting more muddy sludge with every step.

"Mornin', Laura" shouted one of the farmers, busy unloading crates of cauliflowers onto the trestle tables that were standing just in front of his van.

"Morning, Jack, they look like good caulis."

"Oh yes, sittin' in the ground these were, just two hour ago, my love. Not get fresher than that!"

"I dare say not, Jack!" Laura called back as she passed him by.

It was a bitterly cold morning, and she was wrapped up warm with several layers of sweaters under her green Barbour coat to ward off the biting cold. The early morning market had a vibe all of its own. It took a certain type of person to tour the farmers' stalls at 6am looking for the freshest looking vegetables, and negotiating with a hardy bunch of farmers. But this is precisely what Laura had been doing for the last six months since she went into partnership with her old friend Steve and opened up the second of his delicatessens on the opposite side of town. Laura was the only woman in the crowd that congregated at the same time every weekday, but she had soon built up a rapport with some of the farmers, and had developed quite a reputation for keen negotiation. After Steve had

Benefits of Trust

Trust has some very attractive features:

1. It is a resource which increases through use
2. It can enable co-ordination without coercion or competition
3. It enables commitments to be undertaken in situations of high risk
4. It is often held to underpin successful economies
5. A trusted leader is less likely to face challenge and questioning
6. It seems relatively impervious and is therefore a 'deep resource'

Pat Gray author of Policy Disasters in Western Europe

broached the idea of a partnership, Laura volunteered to take the early morning shift to tour the local farms and dairies, collecting the freshest supplies for that day. She knew that Steve had a young family, and so she took the mornings to allow him to spend time with the boys when they got up. This balanced well for her, as she was able to spend quality time most evenings with Tom. She had found unexpected pleasure in cooking dinner for him most nights, often using the meat and produce that she had secured at the market earlier that day. This sense of equality had contributed to the two of them rediscovering their love for each other, and Tom could see that Laura had found her true calling.

Laura loaded up her old van with the crates of produce, and slammed the doors shut. The lock had long since broken – Steve and Laura had bought an old banger from the breaker's yard in an attempt to keep their costs down – and so Laura tied the two handles on the back doors together with some brown yarn. It did the job.

Laura wrapped her scarf tightly around her neck and tucked it inside her jacket. The heater in the van wasn't working and she had one more stop to make at the meat market. She could then make her way back to the new delicatessen that she had opened with Steve on the opposite side of town and get it set up for the day. With her fingers crossed, Laura turned the key and, after a shudder, the engine started. Laura drove the little white van across the fields

TRUST

The smallest word
that makes the
biggest difference.

that surrounded the Farmers' Market, and onto the dirt track on her way to the main road. Ahead of her, she could see the dawn just breaking over the trees. It was a beautiful sight. The mist was just lifting, and the orange glow of the sky gave the countryside a warm, regal quality. It was beautiful.

Laura allowed herself a moment of contemplation as she admired the beauty of the sunrise. Despite the fact that, inside the van, she could see her breath in the cold air every time she exhaled, and her fingers were so cold she could hardly feel them, she was aware of a warm glow deep inside her. It was at that moment that Laura realised that despite being cold, dirty, and more than a little hungry, she was the happiest she had ever been. She was true.

About the Authors

After starting his career with a global engineering company Dan Collins founded *Fresh Tracks* in 1991. Through a combination of innovative training events and consultancy *Fresh Tracks* have helped businesses in sectors as diverse as pharmaceuticals, banking and housing to create better workplaces. The prompt to write *Trust Unwrapped* came from seeing how the best teams seem to operate with high degrees of trust, whilst failing teams always struggle to trust one another.

Dan regularly speaks on issues of teamwork, motivation and trust to audiences around the world.

dan@trustunwrapped.com

David Thompson has been developing people since 1990. During his career he has worked in a number of organisations such as Sainsbury's, Canon, Morgan Stanley, Merrill Lynch, and latterly ABN AMRO, where he held the position of Senior Vice President, Head of People & Organisation Development.

David is the author of a number of books including *Career Helium*, an inspirational story that will change the way you view work. David has also been the teambuilding expert on Channel 4's *Big Brother's Little Brother*, and is a popular speaker and facilitator, with audiences regularly describing his style as 'engaging and entertaining'.

david@trustunwrapped.com

Trust Seminars and workshops can be hosted by the authors and accredited facilitators.

Trust, a 15 minute training film suitable for all audiences, can be purchased or rented from www.trustunwrapped.com

The issue of child labour and chocolate is very real. If you'd like to find out more about which brands are truly ethical and what steps some of the chocolate industry is taking to stop trafficked children being used in the harvest of cocoa then visit www.stopthetraffik.org